The Reference Shelf®

The Two Koreas

Edited by Jennifer Peloso

Editorial Advisor Lynn M. Messina

The Reference Shelf
Volume 76 • Number 3

The H.W. Wilson Company
2004

The Reference Shelf

The books in this series contain reprints of articles, excerpts from books, addresses on current issues, and studies of social trends in the United States and other countries. There are six separately bound numbers in each volume, all of which are usually published in the same calendar year. Numbers one through five are each devoted to a single subject, providing background information and discussion from various points of view and concluding with a subject index and comprehensive bibliography that lists books, pamphlets, and abstracts of additional articles on the subject. The final number of each volume is a collection of recent speeches, and it contains a cumulative speaker index. Books in the series may be purchased individually or on subscription.

Library of Congress has cataloged this title as follows:

The two Koreas / edited by Jennifer Peloso.
     p. cm. — (The Reference Shelf; v. 76, no. 3)
     Includes bibliographical references and index
     ISBN 0-8242-1034-4
     1. Korea (South) 2. Korea (North) I. Peloso, Jennifer. II. Series.

DS902.T86 2004
951.904—dc22   2004048343

Cover: The flags of North Korea (top) and South Korea (bottom). Design by Richard Joseph Stein.

Visit H.W. Wilson's Web site: www.hwwilson.com

Printed in the United States of America

Contents

Preface

Korea is known as the "Land of the Morning Calm" by its people, but history tells a different story, one of tumultuous change and a life full of heartache. A unified country for over 1,200 years, Korea ultimately became a site for occupation by many countries and was subjected to imperial conquests of one form or another over the years. The division of Korea at the 38th parallel after WWII led to a unique situation on the peninsula. Two separate countries emerged, each with its own leadership, economy, way of life, and policies, and each vying for regional power within its sphere of influence. North Korea, with its isolationist policy, has baffled political scientists, while South Korea has, until recently, welcomed an American presence with open arms and has embraced democracy. Korea, a land ravaged by war and plagued by foreign occupation throughout its history, is still torn apart by intrapeninsular tension and animosity even though both North and South are working to ease tensions through diplomacy. This book examines the enigma that is the Korean peninsula.

In the wake of 9/11, a majority of developed and developing countries—with the United States at the forefront—began waging a "war on terror" and sought to rid the world of dictatorial leaders who threatened humanity. In his 2002 State of the Union Address, President George W. Bush named an "axis of evil" that included Iraq, Iran, and North Korea. Even as it was bringing about the demise of Saddam Hussein's regime, the United States was turning its sights toward North Korea and the nuclear threat it now poses to the world after it openly declared not only nuclear capabilities, but also the intentions of using those capabilities against another country should the North Koreans deem it necessary.

The Demilitarized Zone (DMZ) that separates North and South Korea is not only the last vestige of the Cold War, since it was determined by the United States and the Soviet Union at the close of the Korean conflict in 1953, but it is also the most heavily militarized zone in the world. Because only an armistice was signed to ease hostilities between the North and South, a warlike environment still exists along the DMZ. American soldiers make up a large number of the South Korean defense force, and that is why the presence of nuclear weapons in North Korea's arsenal is especially distressing to the United States, whom North Korea has specifically threatened should it feel provoked. Closed to the outside world, North Korea operates within its own bubble, making its activities a mystery to everyone else. It has, however, openly pursued a policy of militarization that has left its economy in a shambles, its people destitute, and its foreign policies lacking, to say the least, all in the name of national defense. The secretiveness and seclusion that North

Korea has sought have alienated it from the rest of the world, and the communist policies it has pursued—the same ones that proved so disastrous to the former Soviet Union—have people in the West asking, simply, Why?

South Korea, on the other hand, has the third largest economy in Asia. Most South Korean homes are internet-accessible; Western technology and culture have been embraced; and democracy constitutes the basis of South Korea's government. With South Korea supporting about 37,000 American troops, anti-Americanism has been on the rise among the younger generation of Koreans who do not remember the Korean War and are pressing for reunification with their northern counterpart. Memories of "The Forgotten War," however, have the older generation wary of reunification and fearful of what the North might do should the United States pull out of South Korea altogether, especially since the North has declared its nuclear capabilities. As the debate over a U.S. presence intensifies, reunification is discussed, and nuclear talks are thwarted, Korea is quickly moving into the international spotlight.

Chapter one of this book focuses on Korea's history and both North and South Korean leadership. Chapter two, "Life on the Peninsula," looks at refugee problems, North Korea's human rights abuses, the reunions organized for North and South Korean families torn apart by the Korean War, and health and education issues facing Korea today. Chapter three examines at foreign relations issues, including how the North and South deal with countries such as Japan and China, the issue of the U.S. presence in South Korea and the generational gap in attitudes over that presence, and the scaling back of American troops along the DMZ. North and South Korea's economies are discussed in chapter four, and chapter five examines both the North and South's military strategies, as well as the questions surrounding North Korea's nuclear capabilities and the threat the country might pose to the rest of the world should it attempt to use the nuclear weapons it insists it has.

I would first like to thank all the newspapers, magazines, and other publications that have given us permission to reprint their work in this book. I would also like to especially thank Lynn Messina and Sandra Watson for their patience and hard work on this book, as well as Richard Stein, Norris Smith, and Gray Young for their help, and Cullen Thomas for his suggestions, insights, and advice.

Jennifer Peloso
June 2004

I. History and
Leadership

Editor's Introduction

To understand a country's present situation, we must first understand its history and the struggles it has faced, for it is often those struggles that define it as a nation. Chapter one provides a brief overview of Korea's eventful history, its various trials, and the diverse ideologies that have shaped the policies and attitudes of North and South Korea's leaders. Although Koreans are highly nationalistic, their history is littered with foreign domination and influence. Molded by the Chinese, shaped by the Japanese, and influenced by the Russians and the Americans, Korea is still learning the true meaning of independence. While it tried for a long time to seclude itself from outsiders, thus earning it the nickname "hermit kingdom," it ultimately fell to imperialism and has yet to thoroughly escape its grip. It is this history of subjugation that informs much of Korean society today.

The chapter begins with a look at the history of Korea prior to and since its division at the 38th parallel. In the first article, "The Korean Peninsula: A Brief Overview of Modern Korean History," Ben Olk covers past and present Korean events, from the country's first alliances with the Chinese and the Japanese, to the Korean War of the 1950s, to the leadership that emerged in the 1990s. The next article, "North Korea: A Political History," focuses on the more enigmatic of the two Koreas, examining the rise to power of Kim il-Sung, "The Great Leader"; the growth of communism in the north; and the impact of these events on the country.

A large part of Korea's history has been dominated by war. Split into two countries after WWII, nothing prepared the Korean people for the political and emotional devastation that would befall them with the onset of the Korean War in 1950. Three long years of intense fighting physically divided families, a people, and their home soil, and memories of that war still influence everyday foreign and domestic relations for both North and South Korea. In the third article in this chapter, "DMZ: Korea's Dangerous Divide," Tom O'Neill examines the effects of the Korean War on the nation and specifically focuses on the establishment of the Demilitarized Zone (DMZ) that divides north and south. After the armistice was signed officially ending hostilities, this area became the most heavily militarized zone in the world. O'Neill looks at the DMZ's structure and layout, the troops stationed along the DMZ, and the tension and attitudes that are ever-present in the minds of soldiers on both sides. The fourth article, by Hamish McDonald, "On the Road to Nowhere," is an account of one man's journey north of the DMZ to gain knowledge about the People's Army and North Korean attitudes about the South and the United States.

Although South Korea has come a long way since its war-torn days of occupation and has established a democratically elected government, it has recently found itself embroiled in political scandals that are rocking not only the country, but also the core of its political system. South Korea's President Roh Moo-hyun was impeached on March 12, 2004, throwing the entire country into political chaos. "Crunch Time for South Korea" discusses the impeachment of Roh, the grounds for his impeachment, and whether or not the impeachment will be upheld by the court, as well as its potential implications for the country's politics, economy, and status in the international community.

While South Korea's leaders are democratically elected, North Korea has been ruled by dictators who can best be described as perplexing, especially to those outside the country. Peter Carlson's "Sins of the Son" examines North Korea's leadership and the Cult of Personality that has run every aspect of daily life since the regime of the "Great Leader," Kim il-Sung, continuing with that of his son, the "Dear Leader," Kim Jong-il. Carlson describes the latter's governing strategies—which have yet to veer away from the harsh policies begun by his father—as he continues to run a state of uncompromising political intolerance.

The Korean Peninsula

A Brief Overview of Modern Korean History[1]

BY BEN OLK
NATIONAL HISTORY DAY, 1997

The history of the Korean peninsula and of its people is full of triumphs and tragedies. Prior to the 20th century, the peninsula had been an independent, united country for more than 1,200 years. For most of that time the Choson or Korean Empire was closely aligned with China. When the Chinese and other East Asian areas became open to Western imperial claims, Korea consciously turned inward. This staunch resistance to foreign influences earned it the name "hermit kingdom." However, seeing the positive developments of its neighbor, Japan, as it underwent the Meiji Restoration—due, in part, to the influence of the West—Korea eventually began to open its borders.

In 1876, the Korean emperor was forced to accept the demands of the Japanese and concluded Korea's first commercial treaty. While the Treaty of Kanghwa overwhelmingly favored the Japanese, it also asserted that Korea was an independent nation, equal to its new trading partner and not a part of the Chinese empire. This clause allowed Japan to intervene in Korean affairs without fear of Chinese reprisal. This marked the beginning of Korea's entry into the world of imperial conquest.

Even though Korea was able to maintain its independence, for the next 30 years, the Korean peninsula would be a prize to be fought over by other powers trying to assert their dominance in the region. The Sino-Japanese War of 1894 was fought after both the Chinese and Japanese intervened in Korea to put down a rebellion in that country. Disagreements over how to withdraw from the peninsula led to the conflict. Eventually, Japan was able to drive the Chinese out, only to have the Russians become interested. During the Russo-Japanese War of 1905, the Japanese again were victorious, and because of a series of agreements made with the British prior to this conflict, they were able gain international recognition of their control over Korea. In 1910, Korea officially became a colony of the Japanese empire. After more than 12 centuries, Korea could no longer boast of its independent stature.

---

1. Article by Ben Olk from 1997 National History Day Curriculum Book Title *Tragedy and Triumph in History.* Copyright © 1997 National History Day. Reprinted with permission.

The era of Japanese colonialism in Korea (1910–1945) is often termed the "dark period." The Korean emperor was replaced by a "resident-general" who maintained dictatorial control over the peninsula. While there were some attempts to rebel against that authority, these were quickly put down.

In typical imperial fashion, all that was done in Korea at this time was done to assist the "mother country." Industries that would benefit Japan were created or enhanced. In agriculture, farmers were forced to do away with the subsistence farming they had been practicing for centuries and moved into a more efficient, single-crop mode that would better support Japan. Koreans were forced to adopt the Japanese culture. Koreans were compelled to use the Japanese language, and, by 1930, all Korean language newspapers were outlawed. Koreans were forced to attend Japanese religious services. Koreans were even "asked" to adopt Japanese surnames. This forced assimilation created bitter feelings between the governed and the governors. That antagonism only increased once the Japanese expanded their empire to include nearly all of eastern Asia beginning in 1931.

Korea was forced to supply the materiel and personnel that would fuel the Japanese war machine. This often meant relocating people to other parts of the peninsula or the empire. By the end of World War II, more than 16 percent of the Korean population had been forced to move in order to accommodate the needs of the Japanese. It is no surprise, then, that the Koreans so enthusiastically celebrated the defeat of their oppressors in 1945.

As the war came to a close, the Japanese immediately turned over their authority in Korea to selected Koreans. These individuals established the Committee for the Preparation of Korean Independence (CPKI), contacting a wide variety of notable Koreans throughout the country. In turn, these leaders established branches of the CPKI ("People's Committees") to assume the control of the governing apparatus. Within three weeks, the CPKI assembled a convention in Seoul, and on September 6, 1945, they announced the formation of the Choson Inmin Konghwaguk, or the Korean People's Republic (KPR). Two days later, the Americans arrived.

In order to hasten the defeat of the Japanese, at the Yalta conference the Allied powers had secretly requested that the Soviet Union declare war on the Japanese 90 days after the defeat of the Germans. On the evening of August 10, Soviet troops began attacking cities on the Korean peninsula. The Americans, aware of the difficulties they had already encountered in Europe with the Soviets, were fearful of complete Soviet occupation of the peninsula; therefore, they proposed that the United States and Soviets divide Korea into two occupation zones. The 38th parallel was arbitrarily set as the boundary between the two. Surprisingly, the Soviets accepted.

The two superpowers differed dramatically in their approach to the newly formed KPR. The Soviets, empathizing with some of the reforms of the people's committees, chose to do very little by way of intervening with the new government. The Americans, however, were much more suspicious of these groups calling for land redistribution and other anti-capitalist reforms. They refused to recognize the new government and immediately replaced it with the USAMGIK (United States Army Military Government in Korea). These initial responses to the KPR set the stage for the two divergent paths that would lead to the creation of two separate countries on the peninsula.

The question of how to create a unified Korean government proved too difficult for the superpowers to answer. Each side began grooming its favorite son to lead a new government. In the north and on the left end of the political spectrum was Kim Il-Sung, a 33-year-old Communist who had spent the war fighting for the Soviet army. In the south and at the other end of the political spectrum was Syngman Rhee, a staunch anti-Communist who had spent most of his adult life in the United States but had been involved in anti-Japanese movements early in his career. Neither man was acceptable to the other side, and all attempts to come up with suitable alternatives failed.

The question of how to create a unified Korean government proved too difficult for the superpowers to answer.

In this context, discussions between the United States and the Soviet Union collapsed. The United States then turned to the United Nations, asking it to supervise elections in Korea. When the Soviet Union objected and U.N. commissioners were refused entry into the North, elections were held only in the South. On August 15, 1948, the Republic of Korea (ROK) was established, with Syngman Rhee as its head. Ten days later elections were held in the North, and on August 25, 1948, Kim Il-Sung proclaimed the creation of the Democratic People's Republic of Korea (DPRK). By 1949, both the Soviet and the American armies had pulled out of their respective zones and the stage was set for a civil war.

While there is no doubt that North Korea was the aggressor on June 25, 1950, it must be noted that there were several short-lived, violent incursions into North Korea prior to that attack. Regardless of who started it, the war itself proved to be a costly standoff between the anti-Communist forces of the U.N. and the Communist forces supported largely by the Soviet Union and China.

Because of the surprise of the attack and the blitzkrieg tactics of the North, the war was almost over before the United States had a chance to get involved. Taking advantage of the fact that the Soviets were boycotting the United Nations because of the U.N.'s unwillingness to recognize the recently victorious Communist government of China, the United States rammed through the Security Council a declaration of war on North Korea. Under the leadership of Douglas MacArthur, the U.N. troops (80 percent of whom were American) dramatically changed the course of the war by executing an amphibious assault on Inchon in September 1948. By November, the allied forces had control of almost two-thirds of the peninsula and appeared poised to unify the whole peninsula under U.N. control.

At this point, the Chinese became involved, and Chinese troops began to pour across the Yalu River in the north. The U.N. troops were forced south again until they could re-establish a front near the 38th parallel. At this point the war settled into a long stalemate. Even though there still existed a tremendous amount of hostility on both sides, by July 1953 they were able to create a cease-fire that still stands today. Although there has never been an official treaty to end the war, this truce agreement has served to maintain an uneasy peace for more than 50 years.

At this point in Korea's history, there is a sharp divide. Little is known of what has taken place in North Korea. We do know that Kim Il-Sung ruled over an oppressive communist regime until his death in 1994. His son, Kim Jong-Il, then was able consolidate his power and took over shortly thereafter.

With its main sources of economic support in the Soviet Union and China having dried up, many experts believe that North Korea has embarked on a course to become a nuclear power. Until 1995, it had refused inspectors entry into several of its nuclear power plants, leading them to suspect North Korea has been squirreling away significant amounts of enriched uranium, which could be used to build nuclear weapons. While there seemed to be some resolution of this issue, most experts believe that enough material could have been produced to create a threatening device. Until the veil of secrecy is removed from this nation, very little else will be known.

In the South, however, we have a better understanding of recent history. While South Korea proclaims itself to be a democracy, it would be a mistake to assume that individuals there enjoy the civil liberties granted to the citizens of most other Western democracies. The pattern that has emerged in this country begins with complete dictatorial takeover of the government, followed by a gradual, slow easing of the restrictions, only to have them abruptly end as a new dictator takes control.

Syngman Rhee moved quickly to consolidate his power in 1948. During this time, with assistance from the United States, Korea began to rebuild its infrastructure. In spite of the economic gains, Rhee's reign was marked by the suppression of all voices of dissent, invoking the fear of Communist takeover to justify his actions. By 1960, the fraud and deception he used to maintain his power could no longer be overlooked by the United States, and in 1960 he was forced to resign.

There followed a brief flowering of democracy, but it was quickly ended in 1963, when a junta led by Park Chung Hee took over. Once again, severe restrictions were placed on the citizenry, and very little opposition was allowed by the Park government. One of the milestones of his administration was the negotiation of the

Normalization Treaty between Japan and the Republic of Korea in 1965. In spite of the historical animus towards Japan, this agreement would set the stage for Korea's economic boom. Millions of Japanese yen poured into South Korea in the form of aid and investment. Japan soon surpassed the United States as Korea's chief trading partner.

By the late '70s, the economy began to slow down and Park was unable to make any significant reforms. In 1979, Park was assassinated by one of his advisers, and once again a brief flowering of democracy occurred. This period ended abruptly in 1981, with the military takeover led by Chun Doo Hwan. In establishing his authority, Chun brutally put down insurrections around the country. Thousands of Korean civilians lost their lives in these protests. Nevertheless, after Chun gained control, he promised to step down at the end of his term in 1987. When he named Roh Tae Woo (one of his co-conspirators in the 1981 coup) as his successor, rioting broke out all over the country. Because the Summer Olympics were due to be held in Seoul in 1988, the rest of the world watched anxiously.

Eventually, Roh Tae Woo made a startling proposal to reform the constitution in order to make it more democratic. This proposal was later accepted by Chun. In the election of 1987, because the opposition vote was divided, Roh Tae Woo won handily. He did, for the most part, live up to the promises he made prior to the election, and South Korea adopted a new, more liberal constitution in 1988.

In the most recent election, Kim Young Sam, one of the opposition candidates in 1987, was able to secure the majority of the votes and became president in 1992. As a result of these reforms, the Republic of Korea has enjoyed a greater degree of democracy for a longer period of time than ever before.

North Korea: A Political History[2]

BBC NEWS, SEPTEMBER 8, 1998

When Kim Il-sung died in July 1994, North Koreans had never known anything else.

The 'Great Leader' had shaped and dominated political and economic affairs for almost half a century.

The outpouring of grief was extraordinary: a product of decades of exposure to a grotesque cult of personality.

Indeed such has been the isolation of this tiny country that it may be many years before North Koreans realise the true legacy of the Kim Il-sung years, and how far and how fast their fortunes have fallen.

Cold War Warriors

The northern half of Korea was born on 9 September 1948 amid the chaos following the end of World War II.

Supported by the Soviet Union, the charismatic Kim Il-sung embarked on a series of popular social and economic reforms, including the redistribution of land and nationalisation of Japanese property.

This gave the communists considerable support, while simultaneously driving many of the skilled and richer parts of the population to the South.

The subsequent Korean War was the result of irreconcilable political differences between Communist North Korea and the U.S.–controlled South.

Neither the Soviet Union, which had occupied North Korea in 1945, nor the U.S.A. could bear the peninsula falling into the other's hands, and the formal division of Korea in 1948 set the stage for military conflict.

The war lasted between 1950 and 1953, causing devastating human losses and eventually more distant relations with the Soviet Union, especially after Stalin's death in 1953.

From Self-Reliance to Self-Destruction

With support from the Soviet Union less assured, Kim Il-sung in the 1950s began a move towards "self-reliance" or Juche.

This led to some industrial success and good economic growth but by the 1970s a combination of higher oil prices and a growing technology gap had undermined the strategy.

---

2. Article from *http://news.bbc.co.uk* September 8, 1998. Copyright © BBC News. Reprinted with permission.

While other communist countries, including China, opted for reform, North Korea maintained the ideological purity of its economic policy but this rigid state controlled system led to increasing problems exacerbated by high levels of military spending.

In 1980, the country defaulted on all of its loans, except those from Japan. By the late 1980s output was declining by more than four percent a year.

But even then Kim Il-sung refused to countenance opening the country to foreign investment or allow private enterprise.

The result has been years of stagnation and an increasingly out of touch leadership, entirely dependent on the cult of personality and increasingly concerned over the issue of political succession.

> ## Economic Decline
>
> - Manufacturing output falling 4–5% annually since 1989.
> - Military spending is 20% GDP
> - Major floods in 1995 and drought destroy many agricultural areas
> - Since 1995, $178.5m of food has been requested through emergency appeals

Power Struggle Follows Kim's Death

When Kim Il-sung died, his son, Kim Jong-Il, took control as head of the armed forces, but did not immediately assume his father's titles of state president and general secretary of the Korean Workers Party. Analysts saw the delay as a sign of weakness.

Rumours of a power struggle were confirmed with the defection of senior ideologue Hwang Jang Yop in February 1997.

Hwang fled to the South Korean embassy while on a trip to Beijing on 12 February 1997.

In the following weeks, the prime minister was replaced and the defence minister died suddenly.

Although accurate information is hard to glean, it now appears that Kim Jong-Il is in control, taking the title of General Secretary of the Communist Party in October 1997. In September 1998 his position as head of armed forces was widened to cover powers of head of state while the post of president was assigned "eternally" to his father Kim Il-sung.

The army remains the main danger to Kim Jong-Il, but he has been careful to woo them since coming to power and he has promoted generals above members of the Korean Workers Party.

He has also promoted a number of relatives: his brother in law Chang Song Taek holds a senior position, as does a cousin, Kim Jong U.

Prospects for the Future

The country's fundamental economic difficulties, its inability to feed itself and the internal political contradictions imply it is no longer a question of if the regime collapses but when.

But a rapid disintegration could have a number of dangers for North Korea's neighbours and for the U.S., which maintains a military presence in the South. A number of scenarios have been discussed.

- A huge wave of refugees could flood across the borders into South Korea, Russia and China.

- Hardline elements could launch a desperate attack on the South. This is known as the 'nightmare scenario' by western planners.

- An internal coup could be launched by disaffected groups in the military or government. The outcome could be hard to predict.

The collapse of the North could lead to a serious escalation of tension between China and the United States. U.S. Defence Secretary, William Cohen, has said that it would be necessary for the 37,000 American troops to stay on after unification.

Such a prospect would cause deep unease in Beijing as would the emergence of a stronger unified Korea.

North Korea remains the world's last outpost of Stalinism. Communist ideology remains strong after years of indoctrination.

The support of China may prevent the country's immediate collapse but there is little sign that the leadership in Pyongyang is ready to embark on any fundamental reforms that could save their people from further misery and turmoil.

Centres of Power

Communist Korean Workers Party: controls all aspects of government. All officials must belong.

Government: led by the president and the Central People's Committee.

The Supreme People's Assembly: the official legislature but has little power. Members elected every four years.

DMZ: Korea's Dangerous Divide[3]

By Tom O'Neill
National Geographic, July 2003

Day eighteen thousand, give or take a few, of the cease-fire
between South and North Korea begins like most other days: Soldiers are preparing for war. In the bitter cold of pre-dawn dark-
ness, 15 South Korean infantrymen huddle together on a road
outside a sleeping farm village and streak their faces with camouflage paint.

They snap magazines of live ammunition into their M4 assault
rifles. With the wind comes a faint strain of martial music, as if
from a ghostly parade, carrying from huge speakers mounted
across the border in North Korea. At a hand signal from the platoon leader, the soldiers noiselessly line up and then disperse,
melting into the surrounding blackness.

Their mission is to patrol a short stretch of the Demilitarized
Zone (DMZ), the contentious no-man's-land that has divided the
two Koreas for 50 years. The bright lights of Seoul, the South
Korean capital, burn less than 35 miles away, but here in the
fenced-off, land-mined, guard-towered DMZ, the only reality is a
shadowy cat-and-mouse game played between soldiers of warring
armies. Every 15 minutes the radioman murmurs the platoon's
position back to the command post: a road, a rice field dike, now
the border itself.

As the platoon approaches a North Korean guard tower, the
leader signals his men to stay alert. If the patrol is particularly
lucky, a North Korean soldier will recklessly dash through the
brush and offer to defect with state secrets. If it is particularly
unlucky, the North Koreans will open fire. That would be unlucky
for all of us: In a worst-case scenario, Korea's uneasy peace could
shatter, spilling war across the peninsula, with millions killed, and
then possibly on to China, Japan, and beyond, pushing the world
toward possible nuclear war.

Apocalyptic thoughts come easy here. In a world full of scary
places—Kashmir, Chechnya, the West Bank—the DMZ is perhaps
the scariest of all, considering the massive firepower deployed on
both sides and the brinkmanship practiced by the rival camps. All
along the 148-mile truce line that bisects the Korean peninsula,
hundreds of thousands of well-trained troops from two of the
world's largest armies (plus more than half of the 37,000 United

---

States troops stationed in South Korea) stand ready to fight, trained by their commanders to hate their ideological opposites and never to let their defenses down.

This state of emergency has persisted since July 27, 1953, when an armistice agreement halted the vicious fighting of the three-year-old Korean War. The origins of the conflict go back to the end of World War II, when the peninsula was split at the 38th parallel by the Soviet Union and the United States as the Allies drove Japan out of Korea. With the tacit consent of its Soviet patron, North Korea launched a surprise, tank-led invasion across the line on June 25, 1950, seeking to impose communist rule throughout the peninsula. China, another freshly minted communist power, entered the war in October, sending waves of soldiers into North Korea when U.N. forces threatened to overrun the Yalu River on the Chinese border. By 1953 almost 900,000 soldiers had died—and more than two million civilians had been killed or wounded—as the South Korean military, joined by United Nations troops composed mostly of American units, battled the forces of North Korea and China to a standstill.

The armistice carved out the DMZ, a 2.5-mile-wide swath of mostly mountainous land stretching across the peninsula near the 38th parallel designed to serve as a buffer zone.

The end of fighting did not bring an end to hostilities. To separate enemies straining at their leashes, the armistice carved out the DMZ, a 2.5-mile-wide swath of mostly mountainous land stretching across the peninsula near the 38th parallel designed to serve as a buffer zone, off-limits to large troop concentrations and to heavy weaponry like tanks and artillery. Straight down its center was drawn the political border, called the Military Demarcation Line (MDL). Then as now, anyone trying to cross the MDL would likely be shot.

To this day, South Korea and North Korea do not recognize each other as sovereign nations. In fact the two Koreas are officially still at war. And often they act like it, keeping tensions sharp as a blade throughout the peninsula and especially along the DMZ.

Recently things have grown dramatically worse. Confronted with U.S. intelligence, the North Korean government last fall suggested that it was secretly enriching uranium to produce nuclear weapons. Early this year it withdrew from the nuclear Nonproliferation Treaty and moved to reactivate a plutonium-reprocessing facility, also to produce weapons material. And then in April, during talks with U.S. officials in Beijing, North Korea asserted that it already possessed nuclear weapons. Did these developments alarm the troops? "Not really," shrugs an American officer stationed just out-side the DMZ. "We can't ratchet up the security any higher than it already is."

Just getting to the DMZ is a challenge. To join the South Korean pre-dawn patrol, I had to pass through several military check-points. One checkpoint guards an entrance to the Civilian Control Zone (CCZ), a high-security belt three to twelve miles wide that borders the length of the Demilitarized Zone. Another checkpoint guards the DMZ itself, right outside Camp Bonifas, one of the westernmost bases along the front line. The 600 South Korean and American troops stationed there provide protection to government officials, military officers, and other guests who come to Panmun-jom, a neutral meeting place inside the DMZ. The troops, known as the United Nations Command Security Battalion, also serve as a thin first line of defense against a North Korean attack. "Some call us a speed bump," Capt. Brian Davis, my escort, says mat-ter-of-factly.

"But if an invasion happens, we'll defend the DMZ and evacuate noncombatants."

Cleared to enter the DMZ and join the patrol, I climb into a Hum-vee, the bulky, all-terrain vehicle of the U.S. military. As we rum-ble northward through the dark with the headlights off, Captain Davis hands me a pair of $3,600 electronic night-vision goggles, standard issue for the forward troops.

In the eerie green glow of the goggles, I see the DMZ fence loom up like a jungle wall—a ten-foot-tall chain-link barrier with a can-opy of coiled razor wire. A rock-hard embankment, erected to stop onrushing tanks, edges the fence on the other side. Beyond that the ground is seeded with mines. Watchtowers crop up every hun-dred yards or so. Except for the areas where steep terrain makes man-made obstacles unnecessary, this bristly fence walls the pen-insula into two irreconcilable halves.

We drive through a gate in the fence, crossing into the DMZ, and soon we sight the platoon as it prepares to set out on patrol. I quickly apply camouflage paint to my face, take a place in the sol-diers' line, and begin walking. An hour into the patrol the sky begins to lighten, causing the soldiers to crouch down and switch off their goggles.

It is a vulnerable time, these moments dividing night from day, and the soldiers wait in their defensive posture for a couple of min-utes until their eyes readjust. We are within sight of the tightly clustered farmhouses in the hamlet of Daeseong-dong, the only South Korean settlement allowed to exist inside the DMZ. No lights shine in the windows. Daeseong-dong's 225 residents live under a strict curfew: off the streets by eleven, confined until dawn.

"Look, there's the enemy," a soldier in front of me says, motioning his head toward a squat concrete guard tower rising up across the MDL less than 50 yards from us. North Korean soldiers in brown uniforms press against its windows, squinting through binoculars and firing off photographs as if we're some kind of wildlife attraction.

"It's OK; we want them to see us," mutters Captain Davis. "These patrols say to North Korea: 'We're here, we're armed, and we're not afraid of you.'"

In the early light we can make out Kijongdong, North Korea's only DMZ village, an orderly collection of buildings fronted by a flagpole 52 stories high, the tallest in the world. A strong, cold wind, compliments of Siberia, barely manages to ripple the huge 600-pound red, white, and blue North Korean flag. *Soldier of Fortune* magazine, I had been told, will pay big money for a piece of that flag.

Our patrol's in-your-face attitude is completely lost on the village: Its population is zero. The fancy-looking apartment buildings are actually flimsy movie-set facades with painted-on windows. Kijongdong, nicknamed Propaganda Village by U.S. and South Korean troops, was built in the 1950s to lure defectors to cross over to the good life in North Korea. So far there have been no takers.

The professed state of war along the DMZ at times also seems weirdly unreal, as if the soldiers are actors at a historical theme park—call it WarLand.

As the sun cracks the horizon, ragged formations of geese and ducks begin to pass noisily above us and swoop down on the fields. The soldiers don't appear to notice. Grimly, silently, they finish the patrol.

The truce has survived another night in the DMZ, and morning brings a sense of peace. But don't be fooled by the quiet, cautions Maj. Kim Bong Su, a senior Korean officer back at Bonifas. "The North Koreans are the same blood as us, but they are the enemy. They always have a gun pointed at my soldiers' hearts."

My first few hours in the DMZ schools me in how the military views the situation: It's good guys versus bad guys, and everyone's trigger finger is itchy. But just as Propaganda Village is not what it appears, the professed state of war along the DMZ at times also seems weirdly unreal, as if the soldiers are actors at a historical theme park—call it WarLand—in a disconnect especially noticeable when civilian life intrudes. Two hours after the South Korean platoon retires to its barracks, tourist buses stream onto the base, delivering giddy visitors eager to buy pieces of DMZ barbed wire strung on plaques and caps emblazoned with the Bonifas motto, "In Front of Them All."

Farmers from Daeseong-dong drift into the rice fields, ignoring their armed escorts as they climb onto threshing machines to resume the harvest. Only descendants of the village's prewar residents are allowed with their families to live in Daeseong-dong. That's where I meet Kim Ok Ja, standing on the edge of a field in a heavy quilted jacket and muddy rubber boots. She first came to Daeseong-dong as a bride, introduced to her husband through a matchmaker. "When I moved here in 1972, I was scared to live so close to North Korea," Mrs. Kim says, watching her husband maneuver the thresher through a field. "I guess I hadn't realized that this was a front line. But I did know that my husband was a good farmer."

A good and affluent farmer. Because of the relatively large farms (roughly 22 acres) and because residents don't pay taxes, Daeseong-dong's farmers earn an average of $53,600 a year, more than twice what rice growers make elsewhere in South Korea. As an added bonus, village boys are excused from military service, mandatory for other Korean males. There's a catch, of course: the nightly curfew, the armed chaperones, and the sporadic threats posed by North Korean infiltrators.

Inside his one-story farmhouse, with radishes and peppers drying on the floor, Kim Kyong Min tells me how a few years back a North Korean platoon kidnapped his mother and brother while they were collecting acorns. They were held for four nights and then released. "We don't know why the soldiers took them," Mr. Kim says. "Thankfully my mother was treated well."

Mr. Kim, a native of Daeseong-dong, betrays no hard feelings about the abduction. He also shrugs off the barrage of music and sloganeering from speakers in nearby North Korea. "I don't even notice it anymore," he laughs. "Let's see what they're saying." He stares into space, listening to the voice coming through his walls. "It says, 'This is paradise. Come over so you can have a good meal of rice.'" He smiles and pours a cup of tea.

Meanwhile in nearby Seoul, a dense high-rise city of ten million, no one, I wager, is staying home this morning out of fear of the 500 North Korean artillery pieces aimed at the city. In fact, last December South Koreans elected as president Roh Moo-hyun, a former labor lawyer who suggested in his campaign that the United States, with its in-country troops and the Bush Administration's "axis of evil" rhetoric, was pushing the two Koreas further apart. Roh's election signaled that many South Koreans want to make up with what they see as an eccentric, gun-crazy, but essentially harmless relative.

Sixteen miles south of the DMZ, inside a bunker with 600 tons of concrete overhead, Capt. Bill Brockman of the U.S. Second Infantry Division is doing a good job of scaring his audience about what lies north of the border. Captain Brockman, dressed in battle fatigues, has invited members of the press to the war room at Camp Red Cloud in the town of Uijeongbu, the division headquarters, for a briefing on North Korea. "We are facing a formidable force, one of the largest militaries in the world," Captain Brockman says. "North Korea has an army of over a million soldiers, 70 percent of them deployed within 12 hours of the border. We're within range of 10,000 artillery tubes. That's enough cannon fire to put Stalin and Napoleon to shame."

For the next hour Captain Brockman describes North Korea's bag of tricks: submarines to sneak troops ashore; infiltration tunnels dug under the DMZ, four of which have been discovered so far; sleeper cells of terrorists inside South Korea; and most frightening of all, 700 to 1,000 ballistic missiles that could be armed with biological, chemical, and possibly even nuclear weapons. North Korea's threat could reach even farther, as it readies long-range missiles capable of reaching the West Coast of the United States.

"Our equipment will dominate theirs in a fight," Captain Brockman says, referring to the advanced weaponry of the U.S. forces and South Korea, with its 690,000 soldiers. "The big advantage the enemy has is its size. They could sweep across the border in successive waves."

What keeps DMZ troops on high alert is North Korea's greatest menace: its unpredictable leader.

Few military analysts expect North Korea to launch a full-scale attack; it would be suicidal, given that the counterattack would likely leave the country in ruins. Another Korean war would cost the lives of hundreds of thousands, if not millions, in the densely populated and economically vital South Korean territory near the DMZ. It would create millions of refugees, even without the use of weapons of mass destruction.

But even if a new Korean War seems unthinkable, what keeps DMZ troops on high alert is North Korea's greatest menace: its unpredictable leader. Kim Jong Il, a secretive and ruthless dictator, presides like a cult deity over one of the world's most closed societies. Under his leadership the country of 23 million people is collapsing economically: Experts estimate that at least 2.5 million North Koreans have died from hunger during the past decade. Yet North Korea diverts most of its scant resources into its military. Because of its inbred hostility to the outside world and because of Kim Jong Il's fear of an attack by the United States, North Korea will likely continue building its huge arsenal, the only bargaining chip it has left to play.

"We literally have a hair-trigger situation that could erupt at any time," Captain Brockman concludes from inside the bunker. "If the North Korean economy collapses, we fear that the leaders may have a use-it or lose-it mentality with their weaponry. So we wonder: Instead of crumbling quietly like East Germany, would North Korea go for broke?" The question hangs in the air like a radioactive cloud. Despite a politically charged atmosphere of saber rattling and dire threats—and notwithstanding all the macho talk tossed around like firecrackers at military camps and guard posts—actual confrontations occur almost exclusively within the half-mile-wide enclave of Panmunjom, the DMZ's "truce village" where the opposing sides come to talk.

The most notorious incident here occurred in 1976 when North Korean troops, upset at a tree-cutting operation near one of their guard towers, bludgeoned two American officers to death with ax handles. In 1984 a 30-minute firefight erupted when North Korean soldiers crossed the line to chase after a defector. Across the DMZ as a whole, a half century of skirmishes has claimed the lives of 90 Americans, 394 South Koreans, and at least 889 North Koreans.

Also called the Joint Security Area, Panmunjom is little more than a collection of no-frills conference rooms bisected by the MDL. Here, 50 years ago, military representatives of China, North Korea, and the United Nations finalized the armistice agreement that stopped the Korean War. Today Panmunjom is the one place in the DMZ where delegates from North Korea and the U.N. Command force meet to discuss military, political, and logistical matters.

You might think, then, that Panmunjom is a decorous, grown-up place. Nope, says Lt. Chris Croninger of the U.N. Command force. "It's like a schoolyard with two bullies poking each other in the eye."

The rules of combat at Panmunjom emphasize mind games—psyching out the enemy. Each side blasts opposing hillsides with patriotic music and recorded messages. A giant signboard on the North Korean side warns—in Korean characters, which few of the Americans can read—"Yankee Go Home." In one of the conference rooms North Koreans once sawed a few inches off chair legs so that their counterparts at the negotiating table would look small and silly. When North Koreans attended a meeting on another occasion with AK-47 assault rifles obviously hidden under their jackets, an armistice violation, American officers chose not to confront them. Instead the Americans took delight in jacking up the room's heat to equatorial levels just so that they could see their adversaries, unwilling to expose their weapons, squirm and sweat in their heavy clothes.

A giant signboard on the North Korean side warns—in Korean characters, which few of the Americans can read—"Yankee Go Home."

Lt. Charles Levine, a lanky South Carolinian who quit a rock band in 1998 and joined the Army, escorts me to Panmunjom to observe the mental war games. The occasion is a "body repatriation," involving the remains of four North Koreans who have washed down rivers into the south. Were they fishermen, soldiers, spies? Levine won't say.

We watch from a window as Red Cross officials from the South pass the coffins to soldiers from the North. But I hardly register the actual transfer. I can't take my eyes off the North Korean guards staring at us through the windows, close enough for us to see the red Kim Jong Il pins on their chests. Their hard stares unnerve me. "As a visitor you are not allowed to gesture at, or communicate with, the North Koreans. They want to provoke incidents," Lieutenant Levine has warned me. That doesn't stop him from shooting dark glances of his own. I also notice Major Kim, the South Korean officer I had interviewed, toeing the Military Demarcation Line—which here is a strip of concrete between the buildings—and glaring like a bad dream at the North Korean soldiers, who glare back.

You wonder if they practice this stuff in front of a mirror. In fact, the soldiers at Panmunjom are chosen for their intimidating appearance. The South Koreans here must stand at least five feet eight, two inches taller on average than their countrymen; a black belt in martial arts is also required. The Americans assigned to Panmunjom are plucked at airports from the batches of GIs arriving from overseas, selected for height—six feet or more is preferred—and for physical bearing. The North Korean sentinels are no slouches either—ramrod straight, steely eyed, and among the best fed people in their famine-threatened country.

Outside the DMZ the big weapons come into play. The mild-sounding Civilian Control Zone, the 590-square-mile restricted area that backs up the DMZ, is bristling with tanks, attack helicopters, rocket launchers, and swarms of soldiers on maneuvers. Inside the CCZ, I sometimes feel as if I've stumbled onto a military coup in progress. Tanks rumble down the main streets of small towns; infantrymen march along country roads followed by jeeps carrying mounted machine guns; soldiers watch from foxholes. No one waves.

Troops and weaponry are concentrated in the farming country north of Seoul, both inside and out of the CCZ, in what are called the Munsan and Cheorwon invasion corridors—broad avenues of level ground that for centuries have served as attack routes to the south. The view from a Black Hawk transport helicopter reveals South Korean Army camps and weapons depots stashed in almost every draw and valley along the edges of the ancient war corridor. The 15,000 U.S. soldiers with the Second Infantry Division are also dug in here, spread out at 17 camps.

For a week U.S. Army personnel whisk photographer Mike Yamashita and me around by van, jeep, and helicopter to see the troops in dress rehearsals for war. One night I watch from a hilltop as sleek Apache helicopters with antitank missiles hover over a village and shoot targets with laser gear. On another day medics practice carrying stretchers under barbed wire as snipers fire on them.

The most intense exercise involves more than 600 soldiers from the 506th Infantry Battalion at Camp Greaves, who are conducting a mock air assault inside the CCZ. Black Hawks drop the troops at night into what the officers called "dinosaur country"—rough, up-and-down terrain—where the men have to clear the high ground of enemy forces (convincingly played by U.S. soldiers with their uniforms turned inside out). A few hours after dawn, a firefight (with blanks) erupts on a nearby hillside. Screams and curses tear through the air as a platoon leader tries to direct his men. Mortars boom and yellow clouds from smoke bombs drift over a greenhouse, flushing out a farmer, a real one, who wants to see why all hell is breaking loose.

No one pays the exasperated farmer any attention. To the soldiers, all civilians look out of place in the security zones, pieces of geography defined and controlled by the military. To the generals the terrain represents a battlefield, pure and simple. Ridgelines offer strategic points from which to shell the enemy. Valleys are invasion routes for tanks. Rivers act as barriers.

In recent times, however, new sets of eyes, civilian eyes, are looking more closely at the DMZ landscape and seeing a very different kind of place. Elderly South Koreans come on weekends to the Freedom Bridge above the Imjin River and gaze longingly across the DMZ to the nearby mountains of North Korea. They see a homeland.

The Korean War split the families of more than seven million people, many of whom fled south during the conflict to escape communist rule. Since 1953 all communication—via mail, phone, or travel—has been cut off by the North. Following a historic summit meeting in 2000, leaders of the two Koreas have allowed brief,

---

> *In recent times, . . . new sets of eyes, civilian eyes, are looking more closely at the DMZ landscape and seeing a very different kind of place.*

---

emotional reunions for 1,200 families. Over 100,000 others have their names on waiting lists. An almost tribal desire for reunification now permeates South Korean society, a legacy of the 13 centuries, ending in 1945, that Korea enjoyed as a unified political entity.

This longing for reunification reaches even to guard posts in the DMZ. In the central mountains, Sgt. Kim Seung Whan, his face streaked with war paint from martial-arts practice, admits that he is uneasy about the prospect of fighting North Koreans. "They are our brothers," he says, "and yet they are our enemies. It is heartbreaking."

Entrepreneurs also eye the DMZ, scanning the lowlands on the peninsula's west and east coasts and seeing corridors for trade and tourism. Recently, both governments have cleared minefields inside the DMZ for two north-south railways closed since the war. In February the first cross-border road in 50 years opened to take South Korean tourists to visit Mount Kumgang, a cluster of sacred peaks in the North.

But the most compelling—and dreamy—vision belongs to conservationists. They look at the wetlands of five rivers crossing the DMZ, and at the Taebaek Mountains, a steep forested maze of 5,000-foot peaks near the east coast, and they see international peace parks, ecosystem preserves, and wildlife sanctuaries.

One of the few good things to come from Korea's 50-year standoff, the security shield erected around the DMZ and its buffer zones has inadvertently preserved the largest piece of undeveloped land— more than 960 square miles—in all of South Korea, one of the world's most densely settled countries. Most of the wilderness remains off-limits, however. To see the DMZ's star wildlife attractions—two species of rare Asian cranes that winter in the Cheorwon Basin—visitors first must apply to the military for permission.

Until tensions ease on the border, which seems a very distant prospect, the only powerful binoculars allowed inside the DMZ will belong not to bird-watchers but to soldiers manning hundreds of guard posts. On a wind-ripped mountaintop in the central DMZ, a South Korean officer hands me his field glasses so I can watch the movements of two North Korean soldiers who have emerged from their guard tower. "They don't have any heat," the officer says. "I think they came outside to get warm in the sun."

In these same mountains a force of one, an amateur wildlife biologist named Lim Sun Nam, helps me finally to see the DMZ as something other than an armed camp. For the past five years Lim, a former TV cameraman, has pursued a quixotic mission to prove the existence in South Korea of the Siberian tiger, the traditional symbol of unified Korea. Tigers officially have been absent from the southern peninsula for at least half a century. But from months of camping and hiking solo in the high country north of Hwacheon, only a few miles south of the DMZ, Lim has found provocative clues: tigerlike prints patterning the snow, tree trunks shredded by large claws, the remains of pigs and cows mauled by a powerful predator, accounts from villagers of hearing roars "like a motorcycle revving."

Lim, a short, powerful man with an Army-style flattop, hurries up a steep hillside, racing the falling sun so he can change the film and battery on a motion-sensing camera. He has positioned it close to where he found several torn-up cows. Lim does not doubt that a family of tigers lives in these mountains. His dream is to convince the military to open a 500-yard-wide gap in the DMZ fence to allow tiger populations from the north and south to meet and breed. But first he must see a tiger and take its picture.

Lim's stories about tigers and their hunting prowess spook me in the gathering dark, my nerves already frayed from living for weeks in the tense surroundings of the DMZ. As Lim camouflages his camera, a bright glow appears at the brow of the hill.

"It's a searchlight," I gasp, certain that the military has arrived on yet another nighttime maneuver. "No, friend," Lim laughs, "that's just the rising of the moon." And suddenly I forget about the DMZ. Tonight we're in tiger country. We're in wilderness. Tonight, for only a moment, we're in a peaceful place.

On the Road to Nowhere[4]

By Hamish McDonald
The Sydney Morning Herald, October 29, 2003

The North Korean army colonel was dismissive of the U.S. victory in the Iraq War, which he had watched closely on television. "It was just a kids' game," he said as the car crossed the North Korean defensive embankment with its tank barriers and electrified fences into the four-kilometre-wide DMZ last week.

"Even though Iraq had some modern weapons, they were not single-hearted, they were not Saddam-centered, and many of their high officials were bribed by the U.S." The colonel was guiding a carload of tourists into Panmunjom, the bizarre village for truce talks set in the middle of the tense frontier that is the Korean demilitarised zone,

Asked whether he was not impressed by America's use of precision missiles, night-visibility goggles and satellite-based targeting, compared with the decade-old Russian equipment that is the best in North Korea's arsenal, the colonel said: "You cannot understand the spirit of the People's Army soldier."

He looked down on the demarcation line dividing Panmunjom, where from just a few metres' distance, People's Army guards were eyeballing their South Korean counterparts, who were wearing sunglasses and standing in clenched-fist taekwondo postures. "They are wearing sunglasses because they cannot stand the fierce gaze of our soldiers," he said. But then the colonel had a question that might have betrayed a certain edginess. "Do you think there will be a war here?" he asked.

How much longer the North Koreans can sustain their formidable conventional forces is one of the big but unanswerable questions swirling around the regional security crisis that broke out when the Pyongyang Government's covert nuclear weapons activity was revealed a year ago.

The answer would reveal how much is invested in nuclear weapons and how easily they could be given up by "the Great Leader, Comrade Kim Jong-Il," the 61-year-old who inherited the regime on the 1994 death of his father, Kim Il-sung.

To the few ordinary foreign visitors, the strain is all too evident. Apart from a few sputtering Chinese and Russian jeeps taking officers to and from the front line, military traffic is absent from North Korean roads. Soldiers hitch rides on passing trucks. There are no condensation trails or jet noises in the sky.

---

4. Article by Hamish McDonald from *The Sydney Morning Herald* October 29, 2003. Copyright © Hamish McDonald. Reprinted with permission.

Though poised in attack positions facing South Korea, the army is static, carefully managing limited stocks of fuel, food and war material. Big parades of military hardware in Pyongyang have been replaced by marching troops and flag-waving civilians.

The economic and human support for the 1.1-million-strong military has visibly crumbled, after the cessation of Soviet aid in the early 1990s was followed by floods that devastated 15 percent of the arable land and wrecked power grids and coal mines, leading to a famine that killed up to 2 million people and is still recalled in persistent stories of cannibalism.

When the four-times-weekly train crosses the Yalu River from the Chinese city of Dandong to the North Korean entry port of Sinuiju, it is a one-kilometre trundle but a time warp of decades. "When I got out on the North Korean station at Sinuiju, it was like going back to the China of the 1960s," said a Chinese passenger on one train last week, after watching whistle-blowing guards keep foreign visitors separate from local people stooped under heavy burdens during laborious passport checks and baggage searches.

The North's industry is operating at 10 to 15 percent capacity because of power shortages and obsolescence.

From the train could be seen teams of children in red and blue tracksuits helping cut the last of the rice harvest with sickles and gather the stalks into bundles. Carts drawn by horses, bullocks and men carried the burdens. Old men and women foraged in hillsides for edible plants. Others picked through harvested fields for heads of grain that had been dropped.

Groups of men panned for gold in a stream. Derelict workshops, abandoned machinery, battered rolling stock and antiquated locomotives could be seen along the railway. According to the South Korean central bank, the North's industry is operating at 10 to 15 percent capacity because of power shortages and obsolescence.

In the train's carriages, senior North Korean cadres in western suits, dark-grey Mao Zedong tunics or the brown twill zip-up jackets favoured by Kim Jong-Il mingled warily with foreigners, their colour-coded Kim Il-sung lapel badges showing they belonged to the higher levels of North Korea's 54-grade political status ranking.

Gazing out at the thin yields of rice and corn and desultory activity, one cadre smoking a foreign brand of cigarette dismissed suggestions that the food supply might be getting better. "You think so?" he asked derisively. "The life of the ordinary people is very difficult. They have to eat what is not natural for people to eat."

At the big Shinanju station, midway to Pyongyang, the results of nearly 20 years of food shortages were plainly seen: groups of stunted young army conscripts who barely made the 1.3-metre minimum height requirement of the People's Army.

In Pyongyang, the capital of 2 million people, which starts abruptly from the countryside with broad empty streets mostly unlit at night and shabby apartment blocks glimmering dimly with low-wattage lights, the people are noticeably better-fed and dressed than those in the countryside.

They ride crammed into trams, trolley-buses and a few smoke-belching diesel buses. High-ranking cadres are driven around in Mercedes-Benz cars; slightly lower ones driving themselves in used Japanese ones.

On one side of central Kim Il-sung Square, the building housing the economic ministries carries the emblem of the Korean Workers Party, the communist party that Kim Jong-Il has sidelined in his cultivation of the military, along with portraits of Marx and Lenin. Last year, Kim belatedly launched his country into a tentative version of China's 1978 market reforms, raising salaries and prices, allowing small markets to open and drastically devaluing the currency from 2.15 won to the U.S. dollar down to 136 won.

The result has been a gradual monetisation of a previously ration- and quota-based economy, but production has not noticeably responded, except perhaps in the numerous small vegetable plots around apartment blocks and workplaces.

Chinese sources who travel often into the country said they were now getting about 100 won to the Chinese yuan, suggesting the North Korean currency is effectively less than 800 to the U.S. dollar and that inflation is spiraling.

Somehow trade with China is expanding, with North Korea's imports surging 22 percent in the first six months of the year to $U.S. 270 million ($383 million), mostly for oil. How it is paid for, when North Korea exported only $U.S. 108 million in the same period, is a mystery unless China is extending endless credit or Pyongyang is using some of the $U.S. 500 million or so it earns annually from its export mainstay, ballistic missiles to the Middle East.

Advertising is absent around Pyongyang, save for political billboards, many showing American forces skewered on People's Army bayonets. Patriotic songs in the style of the Soviet Red Army Choir blare from loudspeakers. Even on the escalators down to the city's Moscow-style underground railway, political commentaries squawk at commuters: "We must safeguard the leadership of Comrade Kim Jong-Il!"

The only other colour comes from portraits of the two Kims, and monuments such as the 170-metre tower topped by a red electric torch erected to commemorate Kim senior's Juche (self-sufficiency) version of Marxism-Leninism, which has been transmuted by his son into an entirely personal or familial cult called Kimilsungism.

That the cult of a dead dictator (now known as the "Eternal leader") continues to wield so much sway over the mind of North Korea is testimony to the regime's propaganda apparatus, the isolation it imposes on the country and a national psyche still trauma-tised by Japan's 1907–45 occupation and the brutal 1950–53 Korean War.

Until the spell is lost, however, it would be unwise to dismiss the colonel's remarks about the fighting spirit of the People's Army.

Crunch Time for South Korea[5]

BY ANDREW WARD
FINANCIAL TIMES, MARCH 15, 2004

For half an hour last Friday morning a collective madness seemed to descend upon South Korea's National Assembly.

Rival lawmakers clashed on the parliament floor as the pro-government party sought in vain to block an impeachment vote against President Roh Moo-hyun. Afterwards, Mr. Roh's supporters flung missiles at the parliamentary speaker before slumping to the floor in tears. Even by the feisty standards of South Korea's fractious democracy these events were shocking.

The impeachment of Mr. Roh, suspending his presidential powers, has created a vacuum in government. The constitutional court is widely expected to overturn the impeachment, meaning Mr. Roh may return to power within a few weeks or months. But for South Korea the loss of political leadership could not have come at a worse time.

The country is entering a critical stage in its development. After more than four decades of rapid expansion, the economy—Asia's fourth-largest—has entered an era of more sluggish growth as competition from China increases. Social divisions are increasing between young liberals and older conservatives. And the country's military alliance with the U.S.—the bedrock of national security— has come under strain as the pair squabble over how to deal with communist North Korea and its nuclear weapons programme.

Last week's political fracas, therefore, is for South Korea part of the wider turmoil of coming to terms with its painful history and an uncertain future. While its newly industrialised economy gives the impression that South Korea is an advanced nation, a deeper exploration of its volatile democracy and corruption-scarred society show it to be a work in progress.

It is true that South Korea recovered from the 1997–98 Asian financial crisis more quickly than other fallen "tiger" economies. Indeed, two years ago its future seemed bright: Seoul's "sunshine" policy of engagement with communist North Korea appeared to be easing military tensions. The optimistic mood was encapsulated in massive street celebrations that accompanied the country's hosting of the soccer World Cup in June 2002, when the national team exceeded expectations by reaching the semi-finals. The achievement appeared to be a metaphor for South Korea's arrival among the ranks of advanced nations.

---

5. Article by Andrew Ward from *Financial Times* March 15, 2004. Copyright © *Financial Times*. Reprinted with permission.

Instead, things have been going wrong ever since. The peninsula was plunged into crisis when the U.S. accused the North of secretly developing nuclear weapons. Meanwhile, the South's economy slumped again as a consumer spending boom ground to a halt.

The seeds of this year's political crisis were sown by Mr. Roh's election as president in December 2002. The left-leaning former human rights lawyer was swept into office by the votes of young, liberal people hungry for reform of South Korea's rigid and conservative society. However, his first year in office was blighted by conflict with an opposition-controlled parliament and infighting within the ruling camp.

Feuding intensified ahead of next month's general election, which will determine the balance of power in parliament for the next four years. When Mr. Roh was criticised by the National Election Committee last month for illegal campaigning on behalf of the pro-government Uri party, his opponents seized on the relatively minor offence as an excuse to impeach him.

Analysts warn that unless the political deadlock is broken Mr. Roh's presidency could turn into "five lost years" for a country that should be moving urgently to stay ahead of China. Some fear the country has hit a plateau with little sign of the momentum needed to reach the next level of development. Annual per capita income has been stalled at Dollars 10,000 (Pounds 5,600, Euros 8,100) for eight years, compared with more than triple that in Japan. Mr. Roh has set a target of doubling the figure to Dollars 20,000 within 10 years. But if he is to have a role in striving for that goal he must first hope that the constitutional court restores his powers, then forge a more constructive relationship with parliament. For that to happen he must either seek compromise with opposition parties or hope the Uri party wins enough seats on April 15 to push legislation through parliament.

Such an outcome is possible: Uri is ahead in the polls and stands to benefit from widespread public anger about the impeachment. But even if Mr. Roh survives this crisis, it is far from clear whether he has the ability to tackle South Korea's many problems.

South Korea's economy expanded by just 3 percent last year—not enough for a country that has enjoyed average annual growth of about 7 percent since the 1960s. Growth has shown signs of recovery this year—driven by strong exports of technology, cars, steel and ships—but the government's 5 percent target could be threatened if the political crisis affects confidence.

Lim Ji-won, economist at JP Morgan, says the political crisis will not have a big impact on the economy because policy is directed by the finance ministry rather than the presidential Blue House. But the longer-term reforms needed to maintain South Korea's competitiveness require strong leadership from the president and support from parliament.

There are two main obstacles to economic reform: the country's militant labour unions, which drive up wages and cause heavy disruption through strikes; and the sprawling, family-owned chaebol or business groups, such as Samsung, LG and Hyundai, that have an unhealthy dominance over the economy, limiting competition and entrepreneurship. Mr. Roh promised to tackle both groups but has made little progress.

Labour militancy is among the reasons why foreign direct investment has more than halved over the past three years. Much of the investment has been lost to China, where labour costs are more than 10 times less. South Korean manufacturers are also moving to China, accelerating the hollowing out of the country's industrial base and increasing unemployment. To remain competitive and create jobs, South Korea needs to develop fresh sources of growth. But investment in areas such as services and science is starved by the concentration of resources on the chaebol, which are hugely powerful in politics and the media.

There are two main obstacles to economic reform: the country's militant labour unions, . . . and the sprawling, family-owned chaebol or business groups.

An ongoing investigation into illegal political fundraising has found that the chaebol donated tens of millions of dollars to politicians before the last presidential election to buy influence. Minority shareholders are beginning to challenge poor corporate governance among the chaebol. But last Friday's failure by foreign investors to oust the fraud-ridden board of SK Corp, part of the third largest chaebol, at a shareholder meeting, showed the degree of resistance to change.

It is in social and institutional reforms that Mr. Roh has enjoyed most success. One of his first acts was to appoint a 46-year-old woman to head the ministry of justice, one of the most conservative, hierarchical and male-dominated arms of government. More independence has been granted to agencies such as the prosecution, tax and intelligence services, which were previously used by presidents as personal instruments of power.

In domestic politics, Mr. Roh set out to eliminate the corruption and regionalism that distort the country's democracy. Revelations that some of Mr. Roh's advisers and relatives received bribes damaged his credibility. But the launching of a wide-ranging investigation into political funding has at least brought into the open the corrupt ties between business and politics. By breaking from the ruling Millennium Democratic party, under whose banner he was elected, Mr. Roh was seeking to smash the regional boundaries that divide the country's politics. The MDP's support is concentrated in the relatively poor and left-leaning south-west, while the conservative Grand National party is based in the industrialised and right-of-centre south-east. By endorsing his supporters' creation of the Uri party, Mr. Roh was trying to create a nationwide reform movement.

Overcoming their traditional rivalry, the GNP and MDP jointly voted for Mr. Roh's impeachment to preserve the old system in which their parties dominated power.

They know that an Uri victory next month could break up their parties and redraw the political landscape—exactly what Mr. Roh, underestimated as a political strategist, set out to achieve.

The struggle between reformists and traditionalists has echoes of the generational upheaval in western Europe and North America in the 1950s and 1960s.

The young are generally contemptuous of their country's old establishment. The fact that young people suffer the highest levels of unemployment is seen as proof that the lack of flexibility in the

---

Many younger people consider the 37,000 U.S. troops in the country as simply the latest colonial power to interfere on the peninsula.

---

country's society and economy creates barriers to talent and ambition. It was Mr. Roh's anti-establishment credentials—his farming parents were too poor to send him to university and so he taught himself to be a lawyer—that encouraged young people and other disaffected parts of society to vote for him in 2002. "We are sick and tired of the corruption and self-interest of our politicians and businessmen," said Lee min-young, an 18-year-old student among an estimated 50,000 people who rallied on Saturday to protest at Mr. Roh's impeachment. Another said: "Mr. Roh has many faults but he is the most honest politician we have ever had. His enemies are scared of that honesty."

However, older heads question Mr. Roh's ability to steer a steady course for South Korea through this turbulent period. They point to the erratic policymaking, weak leadership and frequent expressions of self-doubt that caused his approval rating to fall below 30 percent during his first year in office. With the threat from neighbouring North Korea's 1.1m-strong army, and its own economic and democratic institutions still immature, many believe South Korea needs firm and cautious leadership that an inexperienced maverick such as Mr. Roh cannot provide.

In particular, critics highlight his shaky stewardship of Seoul's alliance with the U.S. as evidence of his unreliability. Mr. Roh was elected on a promise to make Seoul more independent from Washington and improve relations with Pyongyang—exploiting widespread anti-American and pro–North Korean sympathies among young people. While older people remain grateful for the U.S. role in defending the South in the 1950–53 Korean War, many younger people consider the 37,000 U.S. troops in the country as simply the latest colonial power to interfere on the peninsula.

With South Korea's economic ties to China now rivaling those with the U.S.—exports to China exceeded those to the U.S. for the first time last year—some analysts see the Korean peninsula shifting inextricably towards Beijing's sphere of influence.

Mr. Roh's impeachment shows that South Korea's entrenched political and business establishment is still fighting to protect the status quo. But the forces of change in the country's economy, society and foreign relations may now prove inexorable.

Sins of the Son[6]

BY PETER CARLSON
THE WASHINGTON POST, MAY 11, 2003

When the Dear Leader was born in a humble log cabin on Korea's sacred Mount Paekdu in 1942, a bright star and a double rainbow appeared in the sky and a swallow descended from heaven to herald the birth of a "general who will rule all the world."

A soldier in the army commanded by the Dear Leader's father, the Great Leader, saw the star and the rainbow and rejoiced, carving a message into a tree: "Oh, Korea, I announce the birth of the Star of Paekdu."

That's the official North Korean version of the birth of Kim Jong Il, the brutal dictator who rules a nation that now taunts the world with its nuclear weapons. Western historians tell a more prosaic tale: Kim Jong Il was born in an army camp in Siberia, where his father, Kim Il Sung, and his tiny band of communist guerrillas had fled to escape the Japanese.

When it comes to Kim Jong Il, the truth is hard to locate, lost in the thicket of official North Korean mythology and the wild rumors spread by the South Korean media. Does the Dear Leader's presence really cause trees to bloom and snows to melt? Does he really inject himself with the blood of virgins to stay young? Did he really get a hole-in-one the very first time he played golf? Does he really import Swedish blondes to satisfy his lusts?

Probably not. But the reality of Kim Jong Il is at least as strange as the mythology.

The Dear Leader is a pudgy 5-foot-3-inch Stalinist who wears elevator shoes and a puffy pompadour in an unsuccessful attempt to gain stature. Like Hitler, he's an arty aesthete who prefers kitschy artifice to grim reality: While more than a million of his people starved to death in the last decade, he spent billions on gigantic monuments and elaborate stadium spectacles to deify his father and himself. He's a movie producer who says he has always wanted to direct. And he once sent thugs to kidnap a South Korean actress and her director husband so he could force them to help build his country's film industry.

His own bizarre story could make an interesting movie—a surreal epic with drunken orgies, exotic dancing, gourmet pizza, Michael Jordan, a crying contest, magical albino animals and a mummified corpse that reigns as "President for Eternity."

---

6. © 2003. *The Washington Post*, reprinted with permission.

"One of the most interesting questions about Kim Jong Il is: What does it mean to be the son of God?" says Jerrold Post, a George Washington University psychiatrist and a former psychological profiler for the CIA. "It's hard enough to succeed a successful father, but it's quite another thing if the father is elevated to a godlike stature."

Kim Jong Il's father was an uneducated guerrilla who transformed himself into a quasi-divine emperor known as the "Great Leader."

Installed in power by the Soviet army after World War II, the Great Leader, Kim Il Sung, ruled North Korea as a Stalinist dictatorship for nearly 50 years. In 1950 he invaded South Korea. He failed to conquer it, but after four years of war and more than a million deaths, he retained absolute power over his devastated nation, and he proceeded to kill or jail all his rivals, real and imagined.

> *"One of the most interesting questions about Kim Jong Il is: What does it mean to be the son of God?"—*
> **Jerrold Post, psychiatrist**

The Great Leader had an insatiable craving for adulation. By the late '80s he had erected more than 34,000 monuments to himself. His photograph was displayed in every building and pinned to the clothing of every citizen, right over the heart. Benches where he'd once sat were sealed in glass and turned into relics.

Like a king or a Mafia don, the Great Leader groomed his eldest son to succeed him. He dubbed Kim Jong Il "the Dear Leader" and called him "a genius of 10,000 talents."

Apparently, one of those talents was literary. According to North Korean mythology, during the Dear Leader's years at Kim Il Sung University, he wrote 1,500 books—an average of almost a book a day, a feat even Stephen King can't match.

After the Dear Leader graduated in 1964, the Great Leader appointed him to a post in the ruling Workers Party. There, he replaced thousands of old party hacks with young party hacks loyal to him. His rivals tended to disappear.

But the Dear Leader was generous to his supporters. Like Elvis, he gave his cronies cars—generally a Mercedes with an elite license plate number that began with 2–16, after the Dear Leader's birthday, Feb. 16.

When the Dear Leader got a crew cut, supporters did the same. When he let his hair grow and permed it into a puffy pompadour, so did his toadies.

The Dear Leader made no public appearances, but by the early '80s he was running the government behind the scenes.

"Kim Il Sung reigned like an emperor while Kim Jong Il functioned like a prime minister in charge of the day-to-day rule," says Kongdan Oh, a Korean scholar at the Institute for Defense Analyses and co-author of the 2000 study "North Korea Through the Looking Glass."

By all accounts, the Dear Leader's favorite task was running the state propaganda machine, which he gleefully used to deify his father—and, by extension, himself. Today, his picture hangs next to his father's in every building.

"It's a cult of personality like nothing in history," says Oh. "In North Korea, he and his father are like God and Jesus Christ."

The Dear Leader also created a private dance troupe whose performances were racy, at least by North Korean standards. This appalled some of his father's old comrades, including Hwang Jang Yop, the party ideologist who later defected to South Korea in 1997. In his memoirs, Hwang describes his "disgust" with the dances. But, he admits, he applauded with gusto to avoid angering the Dear Leader.

"Are you clapping because you really enjoyed the performance?" Hwang recalls a companion asking him.

"It doesn't matter," he replied. "Just clap like mad. It's an order."

The Dear Leader loves movies.

He has collected more than 10,000 videos. He told an American diplomat that he possesses every Oscar-winning movie. He loves "The Godfather," James Bond flicks, the "Friday the 13th" series, Daffy Duck cartoons, anything with Elizabeth Taylor.

He poured money into the state film company, made 341 officially recorded visits to its studio, commissioned a 100-part serial on North Korean history and wrote a book called "On the Theory of Cinema Arts."

He frequently demands—and of course receives—screen credits.

"Kim Jong Il can claim credit—I wrote it, I directed it—but it is lies, of course," says Kongdan Oh.

The Dear Leader is a keen appreciator of cinematic talent and he's willing to do whatever it takes to get stars—even kidnap them.

In January 1978, while South Korean actress Choi Eun Hee was visiting Hong Kong, several men grabbed her and carried her, screaming and sobbing, to a freighter. When the ship landed in North Korea, the Dear Leader stood waiting on the dock.

"You have suffered a great deal trying to come here," he said. "I am Kim Jong Il."

She was driven to one of the Dear Leader's villas and held under guard. Her husband, Shin Sang Ok, a prominent South Korean producer and director, was searching for her in Hong Kong when he, too, was abducted, knocked out with chloroform and shipped to North Korea.

For five years they were held captive—Choi in villas, Shin in a prison—with no knowledge of each other's whereabouts. Finally, in 1983, the Dear Leader theatrically reunited them at a banquet at party headquarters. He apologized for kidnapping them, begged forgiveness and asked them to make movies for him.

When they agreed, he set them up in a luxury home, gave them matching Mercedeses and invited them to wild parties where naked dancers cavorted with drunken party bosses.

Over the next two years, they made seven movies for the Dear Leader. One of them, *One-Way Mission*, won the best director award at a Czech film festival in 1985. The Dear Leader was thrilled.

A year later, while traveling to Hungary, they escaped from their guards in Vienna and fled to the American Embassy. Stashed at a CIA safe house near Washington for two years, they wrote a memoir that became a huge bestseller in Asia, then moved back to Seoul.

In interviews, they were surprisingly kind to the Dear Leader. Sure, he drank too much, cheated on his wife and humiliated his underlings, they told reporters, but he was also smart, funny and hard-working—a man who would make a great Hollywood producer.

Choi told a story that made the Dear Leader seem almost charming: One day, he came for a visit and asked, "What do you think of my physique?"

She hesitated, pondering how to answer such a question when it comes from a short, dumpy dictator known to execute his enemies.

"Small as a midget's turd, aren't I?" he said, smiling.

"Entering 1994, Kim Il Sung looked fine on the surface," wrote Hwang Jang Yop in his post-defection memoir, "but considering the fact that he could not even control his flatulence when talking to us, I started to believe that his days were numbered."

Hwang was right. On July 8, 1994, the Great Leader died of a heart attack at 82.

His death caused a flood of tears. Tens of thousands of Koreans flocked to statues of the Great Leader and wept uncontrollably. They cried, they keened, they wailed. Many fainted, several suffered heart attacks.

It was a genuine outpouring of grief by the people, but among the party elite, Hwang reveals, it soon became a contest to see who could cry most.

"There started an open competition of crying," he wrote. "One might cry once or twice but there is no way to keep on crying. But since people had to continue paying respects to Kim Il Sung's body, or offering flowers at his statue, they just pretended to cry, holding a handkerchief to their eyes."

The orgies of weeping inspired a new myth for the cult of Kim, and it was soon featured in a propaganda film.

"When the most beloved leader Kim Il Sung passed away, thousands of cranes descended from heaven to fetch him," the narrator intones mournfully over shots of cranes flying through gray skies. "But the birds couldn't take him away because they saw that all North Koreans cried and screamed and pummeled their chests and pulled out their hair."

Deeply moved, the cranes instead put Kim Il Sung to rest "in a heavenly palace built on Earth."

That "heavenly palace" is the Great Leader's Kumsusan Palace, which the Dear Leader renovated—for an estimated $900 million—into an elaborate tomb. There, the mummified corpse sits under glass, reigning as "President for Eternity."

At the Great Leader's funeral, there were many eulogies but Kim Jong Il did not say a word.

> **The Dear Leader rules a country in ruin.**

The Dear Leader is not a great orator. In fact, he is not an orator, period. Before his father's death he had uttered only one sentence in public. It came in 1992, at a celebration of the North Korean army: "Glory to the people's heroic military!"

After the funeral, diplomats waited for an announcement that the Dear Leader had taken over the Great Leader's job. No announcement came.

There were hints. The foreign minister declared: "The Dear Leader is the Great Leader and the Great Leader is the Dear Leader." The new party slogan became: "Kim Il Sung is Kim Jong Il."

Korea watchers predicted that the announcement would come after a 100-day mourning period. It didn't. They predicted it would come after a one-year mourning period. It didn't.

The silence from the capital of Pyongyang inspired endless speculation in the Western media: Kim Jong Il was sick. Or he'd been injured in a car accident. Or he was mute. Or he was battling rivals for power.

Around the world, journalists wrote profiles that recycled all the old rumors about Kim Jong Il:

He's a drunk who buys more Hennessy's top-of-the-line cognac than anyone in the world. He's a womanizer who employs "pleasure squads"—perhaps blondes imported from Sweden—to satisfy his depraved lusts. He's a basketball fan who loves Michael Jordan. He has an IQ of 150. He's phobic about germs. He surfs the 'Net.

The Dear Leader was (and remains) unavailable for comment.

"Kim's apparent unwillingness to consummate the succession," a Korea expert wrote in a scholarly publication in 1996, "is slowly driving policy wonks out of their minds."

Finally, in September 1997, North Korea's official news agency reported that a spontaneous groundswell of popular opinion had compelled the Workers' Party to elect Kim Jong Il to rule the nation.

This momentous event caused pear trees to bloom in autumn. And fishermen netted a rare albino sea cucumber—a marine animal that had come to hail the Dear Leader's triumph.

"Seeing the mysterious natural phenomena," the news dispatch continued, "Koreans say that Kim Jong Il is indeed the greatest of great men produced by heaven."

The Dear Leader rules a country in ruin.

Battered by floods, decades of mismanagement and cutbacks in aid from the former Soviet bloc, the North Korean economy collapsed in the 1990s. Factories closed, offices went unheated, electricity flickered on and off. In the countryside, peasants ate grass and bark.

"If you went a little outside the center of Pyongyang," Hwang Jang Yop wrote in his memoir, "the roads were filled with people who were reduced to mere skeletons."

At least a million of North Korea's 22 million people starved to death.

The Dear Leader was not unmoved. He responded to the famine by executing his agriculture secretary.

In a rare speech in 1996, he said the starvation wasn't his fault. "The Great Leader told me when he was alive never to be involved in economic projects," he explained, "just to concentrate on the military and the party and leave economics to party functionaries."

He did not promise to feed his people but he did promise to feed his million-member army. "If the U.S. imperialists know that we do not have rice for the military," he said, "then they would immediately invade us."

A fat man in a famine, the Dear Leader also took steps to guarantee his own supply of food, including pizza. In 1999, his agents recruited two Italian chefs and brought them to North Korea, where they set up a state-of-the-art pizza kitchen and trained the Dear Leader's cooks in the fine points of gourmet pizza—a bizarre episode that one of the Italians, Ermanno Furlanis, later recounted in an article titled "I Made Pizza for Kim Jong Il."

The Dear Leader's personal life is a soap opera wrapped in an enigma.

His father was a tyrant who thought he was God. His mother died when he was 4, and a year later, he saw his brother drown in a pond.

His father remarried and, if we can believe the accounts of defectors, the Dear Leader hated his stepmother and cut her face out of family photos. He also resented his stepbrother, who was more handsome and popular. As soon as he acquired power, he shipped the stepbrother off to diplomatic posts in places like Bulgaria.

The Dear Leader fathered four children by four women. Or maybe it was three children by three women. It depends on which account you read. North Korea lacks a *People* magazine to sort these details.

His first wife was an actress named Song Hye Rim, star of the North Korean movie "Village at the Demarcation Line." She was married when they met, but the Dear Leader sent her husband off to France. In 1971, she gave birth to the Dear Leader's eldest son, Kim Jong Nam, but the marriage fell apart and she moved (or was sent) to Moscow, where she died in 2002.

Her niece and nephew defected, and they entertained interviewers with stories of the dysfunctional Kim family—at least until the nephew was murdered in South Korea, allegedly by North Korean agents.

Meanwhile, the Dear Leader and his various women produced another son and a daughter—or maybe two daughters. His current wife is a former dancer named Ko Young Hui, the mother of the Dear Leader's second son, Kim Jong Chol, 22.

In 2001, the Dear Leader's eldest son, Kim Jong Nam—presumed heir to the throne—was arrested trying to enter Japan on a fake passport from the Dominican Republic. Accompanied by two women and a 4-year-old boy, he was wearing a Rolex watch and carrying a fat wad of money. Questioned by customs officials, he offered a simple explanation. "I wanted to go to Disneyland," he said.

All this family drama and trauma could drive a man crazy. And Jerrold Post, the GWU professor and former CIA psychiatrist, believes that the Dear Leader has a serious mental illness.

"He has the core characteristics of the most dangerous personality disorder, malignant narcissism," Post theorized in a recent psychological profile.

The disorder is characterized by self-absorption, an inability to empathize, a lack of conscience, paranoia and "unconstrained aggression."

The Dear Leader, Post concluded, "will use whatever aggression is necessary, without qualm of conscience, be it to eliminate an individual or to strike out at a particular group."

In 1998, the Dear Leader's army launched a Taepo Dong ballistic missile that flew over Japan and plopped into the Pacific Ocean.

That act frightened North Korea's neighbors, who were already nervous over reports that Kim Jong Il was secretly building nuclear weapons.

In January 2002, President Bush denounced North Korea as part of the "axis of evil"—a rogue regime "arming with missiles and weapons of mass destruction." North Korea responded by calling Bush's statement "little short of a declaration of war" and promising to "mercilessly wipe out the aggressors."

In October 2002, the Dear Leader's government admitted that it was taking steps toward building an atomic bomb. American officials said they suspected that North Korea might already have a nuke or two.

In December 2002, while United Nations weapons inspectors watched, North Korean officials theatrically opened a nuclear reactor that had been sealed for a decade and celebrated with a round of beers. Then they kicked the U.N. inspectors out of the country.

In March 2003, the United States invaded Iraq—another member of the "axis of evil"—and the Dear Leader's government responded that the invasion proved that "to prevent a war . . . it is necessary to have a powerful physical deterrent."

In April, American newspapers reported that Defense Secretary Donald Rumsfeld was circulating a memo proposing that the United States and China team up to oust the Dear Leader's government.

A week later, a North Korean official negotiating with Americans in Beijing announced that his country has nuclear weapons and threatened to either export them or conduct a "physical demonstration."

A few days later, North Korea announced that it would regard any American attempt to impose economic sanctions as "the green light to a war."

It was frightening—an escalating war of words that threatened to explode in a hellish nuclear holocaust.

On the other hand, there was one brief ray of hope. On February 16—the Dear Leader's 61st birthday—North Korean television announced that the appearance of a rare albino raccoon was a sure sign of good times ahead.

> *North Korea announced that it would regard any American attempt to impose economic sanctions as "the green light to a war."*

"He was not some hysterical crazy person," says Wendy Sherman. "He was very polite. He had things he wanted to say. He didn't work from any notes or talking points. He had tremendous confidence."

Sherman—who was special adviser to the president on North Korea during the Clinton administration—is one of the few Americans who have met Kim Jong Il. She spent two days with him during Secretary of State Madeleine Albright's diplomatic mission to North Korea in 2000.

Albright presented the Dear Leader with a gift—a basketball autographed by Michael Jordan. They posed for pictures, then sat and talked for a while.

"He told us he had a surprise for us for the evening's entertainment," Sherman recalls. "He had something he wanted to take us to."

The Dear Leader escorted them into a huge stadium. When they entered, a crowd of more than 100,000 roared. "For five or 10 minutes, people just cheered him and chanted his name," she says. "It was just amazing."

The Dear Leader waved. Fireworks exploded overhead. Dancers waved flags and pompoms. Acrobats rolled in hoops. For hours, thousands of colorfully costumed performers acted out scenes with such titles as "If the Party Decides, So We Do."

The Dear Leader said he'd helped to choreograph the show himself.

In the stands, 25,000 people flipped colored cards depicting elaborate scenes. One showed the Dear Leader's Mercedes driving through amber waves of grain. Another showed the launch of the Taepo Dong missile that terrified Japan in 1998.

"It was sort of a Super Bowl halftime show writ large," Sherman says.

The next night, the Dear Leader hosted a state dinner that was followed by another show, this one less elaborate but still impressive.

Sherman turned to the Dear Leader. "Mr. Chairman," she said, "I get the impression that in some other life, you were a director."

"Oh, yes," he said, beaming. "I love directing! I love the theater!"

Cult of Personality*

VIRTUALVOYAGER

A cult of personality is a generally derogative term to criticize the worship of a single leader.

Personality cults are usually characteristic of totalitarian states, or post-revolutionary nations. The reputation of a single leader, often characterized as the "liberator" or "savior" of the people, is glorified to an almost divine level. The leader's picture is displayed everywhere, as are statues and other monuments to his greatness and wisdom. Slogans of the leader are plastered on massive billboards, and books containing his speeches and writings fill up the bookstores and libraries.

The goal of a personality cult is to make the leader and the state seem synonymous, so it becomes impossible to comprehend the existence of one without the other. It also helps justify the often harsh rule of the dictatorship, and propagandize the citizens into believing the leader is a kind and just ruler.

The creation of such a vast cult is often used in particular as a criticism of the regimes of Joseph Stalin and Mao Zedong. During the peak of their reigns both leaders were portrayed as god-like omniscient rulers who were destined to rule their nation for all eternity. Their portraits were ordered to be hung in every home and public building, and many artists and poets were only allowed to produce works that glorified the leader. To justify this level of worship, both Mao and Stalin tried to come off as humble and modest and would often characterize their vast personality cults as nothing more than a spontaneous show of affection by their people. Stalin in particular used this excuse to justify the Communist Party's massive campaign of renaming things in his honor.

Other notable past personality cults included that of Kemal Ataturk's Turkey, and Saddam Hussein's Iraq.

Some current nations that feature personality cults include Saparmurat Niyazov's Turkmenistan and Kim Jong Il's North Korea.

It is important to note that a cult of personality is not necessarily universal among all totalitarian societies. In a few situations there have been cases in which it is more beneficial to the regime for there to be little to no worship of the leader. For example, the Khmer Rouge and the Taliban were lacking in cults of personality and the leaders in these regimes were almost anonymous.

---

*This article is licensed under the GNU Free Documentation License (*www.gnu.org/copyleft/fdl.html*). It uses material from the Infovoyager article "Cult of Personality" (*ruv.net/infopedia/cu/Cult_of_personality. html*).

II. Life on the Peninsula

Editor's Introduction

As North Korea declares its nuclear capabilities, South Korea grows more anti-American, and rumors of possible reunification surface, the international community is forced to take greater notice of Korean affairs. Once known as the "Hermit Kingdom" due to its reclusive behavior, Korea has become a political hot-spot in recent years. Nevertheless, politics is not the only pressing issue facing the peninsula today. A number of domestic issues shape everyday life in Korea, and several of them are discussed in chapter two.

Life is not easy for North Koreans, who are plagued by starvation and human rights abuses perpetrated by Kim Jong-il's regime. It is estimated that over 1 million people in the North have died of starvation in the last half-decade, and the human rights abuses inflicted upon the North Korean populace rival those found in Nazi Germany's concentration camps during WWII. It is these abuses that force many North Koreans to become refugees and flee to China in the hopes of a better life. The first article in this chapter, "Escape from Hell" by John J. Miller, focuses on the refugee crisis that plagues North Korea. Miller not only discusses China's role in this crisis and its reluctance to risk damaging the precarious relationship it has with North Korea by accepting its refugees, but he also examines the U.N.'s avoidance of the North's refugee situation and the blind eye the U.N. has turned towards China's handling of it. Miller also reports on some of the specific abuses inflicted upon the population—witnessed by the few North Koreans who actually made it out of the country and now devote their time to educating Westerners about the atrocities that occur there daily.

Basic human needs may be driving North Koreans to attempt a dangerous border crossing, but in a democratic society like South Korea, decisions for emigrating are quite different. Jeremy Garlick, in "Flying Toward New Dreams," discusses some of the reasons—such as population density, age and gender discrimination, and education—that cause South Koreans to contemplate an international move.

While some Koreans are willing to leave their families to seek a better life elsewhere, many are more interested in reuniting with family members from whom they were separated by the Korean War and the DMZ, which was established afterwards. Movement across the DMZ has been forbidden, thus tearing apart many families who have not seen each other in over 50 years. As diplomatic relations between the two countries have recently resumed and tensions have eased, one of the top priorities for many Koreans has been reuniting families. In her article "50 Years Later, Reunions Bring Joy to Koreans," Stephanie Strom discusses the events surrounding family reunions and the diplomatic reasons on both sides for allowing such reunions to take place.

Reuniting families is only one means by which North and South Korea have attempted to promote peace and end the hostility that has characterized their dealings with each other for over 50 years. Tensions between the two countries had begun to ease in the 1970s with the introduction of the Sunshine Policy, the concept for which was developed by South Korean president Kim Dae-jung, based on the moral of one of Aesop's fables. "International Support a Key to Korean Peace" by Jeong Se-hyun discusses this policy that broke the ice and reestablished friendly relations between North and South. Se-hyun describes the goals of the policy, what has been done to realize those goals, and what must still be done to achieve peace.

With relations between the two countries improving, talk of reunification has increased, and William Dawkins considers the implications of such a union in "Detente Could Unsettle Balance of Power." Dawkins examines the pros and cons of reunification, focusing mainly on the distribution of influence among nations in the region and how that balance could potentially be affected by a unified Korea. Dawkins says that while many are pushing for reunification, others are wary of it; he explains the reasons surrounding their anxiety.

As is the case around the world, one of the most important issues facing Koreans today is health care. Though little is known about North Korea's health care system, due to its decision to remain a closed society, the world is becoming acutely aware of the widespread starvation and malnutrition currently facing its people. Barbara Demick addresses these concerns, which are beginning to cause alarm outside of the peninsula, in her article "A Small Problem Growing."

Escape from Hell[1]

BY JOHN J. MILLER
NATIONAL REVIEW, JANUARY 27, 2003

Kang Kil-Ok knew she had to flee North Korea after security guards beat her 61-year-old mother so badly that the old lady couldn't walk.

It was the summer of 1997. Kang's brother and his family had vanished. One suspicion was that the regime of dictator Kim Jong Il had taken them away, to a prison camp or some other terrible fate, for a crime they may or may not have committed. With government officials quizzing the relatives, however, the disappearance could really mean only a single thing: The family had fled to China, and the agents wanted to track them down.

They figured Kang's mother would know something, and they were determined to beat it out of her. "After the interrogation, my mother's knees were so badly bruised, she couldn't even stand up. They kicked her with boots and whacked her with sticks," says Kang. Her mother died a few months later. "How could they do such a thing to a 61-year-old woman? It made me realize that I had to leave North Korea, too."

And that's what Kang did, in a four-year ordeal that had her crossing the border under gunfire, resisting pressure to become a prostitute, accepting a sham marriage to hide from Chinese police, and finally escaping to freedom in South Korea. Parts of her story are hardly unique—indeed, they are disturbingly common—but they also illuminate the horrible reality of North Korea, as well as the dangers North Korean refugees face in China, where the government is committed to rounding them up and returning them to a country whose penal code lists defection as a capital crime.

Nobody knows how many North Koreans have tried to escape from the shackles of Kim Jong Il's totalitarianism, but some estimates put the number of North Korean refugees now hiding in China as high as 300,000. They've fled from a ruthless machine of political terror, and from a failed system of economics that has starved 2 million people to death—out of a population totaling 22 million—and left many more malnourished. Very few of these refugees have made it out of both North Korea and China. But those who have escaped have riveting stories to tell, as they bear witness to life and death under what may be the world's most oppressive government and its Chinese ally.

The Gulag State

Kang Kil-Ok is now 32, and lives in Seoul. Her interview with *National Review*, conducted by phone and with a translator, is the first she's given anywhere. Yet even now she can't operate outside the long reach of Kim Jong Il; under North Korea's collectivist philosophy, whole families may be punished for the alleged crimes of individual members. This form of social control stops many North Korean defectors from telling their stories at all, and keeps others from revealing their true identities when they do. "Kang," therefore, is an alias.

"After they tried to make an example of my mother, everything changed. People started keeping their distance. My boyfriend stopped seeing me," says Kang. She worked long hours at a gunpowder plant, lived in a dormitory building, and often lacked food. "I became very depressed." She also learned for certain that her brother had taken his family to China—he sent her a letter that included details on how to contact him if she were to make it out as well. "I couldn't wait any longer. If the government found out that I knew he was in China and hadn't told them, I would be thrown into a prison camp."

> *"If the government found out that I knew he was in China and hadn't told them, I would be thrown into a prison camp."*—Kang Kil-Ok

This was something to avoid at all costs. The stories from North Korean prison camps, as recounted by the handful of survivors who have managed to escape them, rival the stories from Nazi concentration camps and the Soviet Gulag. One of these survivors, Sun-ok Lee, testified at a congressional hearing last May. She had once run a government supply office in North Korea, but was accused of embezzlement and sentenced to prison. The days were full of hard labor, and even the nights brought no relief: "Some 80 to 90 prisoners sleep in a flea-infested chamber about six meters long by five meters wide (about 19 feet by 16 feet). . . . The prison chamber is so congested that sleeping there is itself a torture."

Prisoners charged with additional crimes, such as failing to meet work quotas or not memorizing the president's New Year message, are confined in "punishment cells"—spaces so small it's impossible to stand up or lie down. The cells are so awful, reported Lee, that "it is a day of great fortune if a prisoner finds a rat creeping up from the bottom of the toilet hole. The prisoners catch it with their bare hands and devour it raw, as rats are the only source of meat in the prison." But they have to do their rat feasting on the sly: Getting caught lengthens their sentences.

The testimonies of prison-camp survivors are full of such wretched tales; among the worst are those dealing with pregnant women. Young-Hwa Choi, a North Korean who made it to Seoul last March, recently told a rapt audience at the American Enterprise Institute about a woman she knew in prison. Her friend had fled to China and become pregnant, but then was caught by the police and repatriated to North Korea, which promptly threw her into prison. As she approached her due date, she was taken to a hospital; Choi was allowed to accompany her. Choi tells what happened next: "They put a towel on the face of the baby right after birth, right before the mother. They said, 'Any Chinese seeds have to be eliminated.'"

Sun-ok Lee tells a similar story from her time in prison. She was ordered to a medical room to help with some record-keeping. Six pregnant women were there. "It was horrible to watch the prison doctor kicking the pregnant women with his boots. When a baby was born, the doctor shouted, 'Kill it quickly! How can a criminal in the prison expect to have a baby? Kill it!'" In the presence of the mothers, reports Lee, the babies' necks were squeezed until death came. Other witnesses to infanticide report that prison guards sometimes make the mothers themselves do the killing.

This was the kind of fate Kang dreaded when she learned of her brother's whereabouts in China, so she started to plan an escape. She knew of a local woman familiar with the human-trafficking networks that emerged during the famines of the 1990s. The hunger problem has eased slightly, but the exodus has only increased, because people have developed an effective underground railroad into northeast China. Some of its operators are Christian missionaries motivated by humanitarianism; most of the traffickers, however, just want to make money, and the woman Kang contacted was one of these. She agreed to help Kang get across, and Kang agreed to pay the debt with the income she would earn working in China.

And China is where refugees have to go, because North Koreans can't simply walk across the border into South Korea. The DMZ separating the two countries is one of the most militarized places on the planet. Even if all the troops were to leave, the huge number of landmines would make it a perilous crossing. For most North Koreans, then, escape means passage into China across a cold river patrolled by border guards. There are bribes to be paid and eyes to be averted. The Tumen River dividing North Korea and China isn't especially broad or deep and may be waded at many points, but its waters are frigid. As one refugee told Human Rights Watch, "I endured the coldness, even though it was as painful as cutting my flesh with a knife." Many refugees prefer to cross in the winter, when the river freezes.

That was Kang's plan, and it seemed a good one for the month of December. But the ice was thin, and it cracked beneath her feet. Kang and her companion, the trafficker, splashed into the water.

Border guards heard the commotion and started yelling at them to come back. Kang was confused; these men were supposed to have been paid off. "Ignore them," shouted her guide. "Just keep going." Kang pressed on in the cold. Shots rang out, but she continued forward. "Somehow, we made it to the other side," she says.

For many refugees, getting out of North Korea is the easy part, because China is no safe haven for them. Helie Lee, the Korean-American author of the best-selling book *Still Life with Rice*, said in Senate testimony last year that a bribe of about $400 was enough to get nine of her kin past the border guards—but getting them out of China was so perilous that each of them carried enough rat poison to commit suicide. (Lee describes their difficulties in a more recent book, *In the Absence of Sun.*)

The problem is that China wants to prop up North Korea's regime—partly as a check against American power in the region, but also because its collapse would lead to a massive and unwanted migration into China. Everybody who watches the North Korean situation draws parallels between what's happening there right now and what happened in Eastern Europe in the late 1980s, when Czechoslovakia and Hungary opened their borders to East Germans and precipitated the destruction of the Iron Curtain. China wants to avoid this result, and so it hunts down the refugees hiding within its borders and forces them back to North Korea.

Human Cargo

The North Koreans in China stick out the way Mexican peasants do in Phoenix. Their dress is often a giveaway, and so are their physical features—many have dark or blotchy skin from vitamin deficiencies. Few of them speak Chinese, and they must rely on the many Korean-speakers on the Chinese side of the border. (Northeast China is full of ethnic Koreans, and many people have relatives in both countries.) During another famine sparked by the failures of Communism—Mao's "Great Leap Forward," 1958–61—many Chinese actually fled into North Korea, seeking assistance. With migrants flowing the other way, there's a latent sympathy for their plight. There's also plenty of exploitation. Employers know that refugees will work for about half the wages of Chinese nationals. The North Koreans may also be held for ransom, if they have family able to pay for their release. The women are often forced into prostitution, or sold as wives—which is what happened to Kang.

After crossing the river, Kang walked to a Chinese city with her trafficker. She changed clothes and was taken to a house, where a group of ladies welcomed her. They fed her, gave her a room and a bed, and let her have some rest. "Then they pushed me to accept a man—they wanted me to become a whore," says Kang. "I told them that I came to China to look for my brother, not to sell my body." She struck a deal with her keepers: They would give her a day or two to track down her brother and get him to pay for her release. If she failed, she would become a prostitute.

Kang called a phone number her brother had given her, and he told her to stay put. He sent friends, and they assured Kang's guide that she would be paid if they all traveled to a nearby city. She agreed, and the group embarked on a bus. The Chinese had set up a police checkpoint on the way; Kang and her companions fled into the wilderness. Eventually they made it to their destination, and Kang was reunited with her brother, her niece, and her grandmother. But complications arose over payment, and the trafficker threatened to report the family to the Chinese police. "I'm a dead body here or in North Korea," Kang told her. "If you report me, I'll get you, too." The trafficker fled.

It's hard to blame the human-cargo traffickers for wanting to make a little cash. North Korea's economy is moribund, with a landscape full of empty factories and idle trucks. The worst part of the grinding poverty is the hunger. The North Korean government likes to treat the deadly famines of the 1990s as the result of unavoidable natural disasters, but there were problems even before these struck. When the 1992 harvest showed poor results, for instance, the government promoted food rationing and relied on

> *The vast majority of North Korean refugees don't see themselves on an ideological trek to the West; . . . they just want to feed themselves.*

a propaganda program with a belt-tightening message: "Let's Eat Two Meals a Day." Whereas another regime might have started to think about introducing market principles to alleviate the hunger, Kim Jong Il recoiled at the thought. Unlike his father, the "Great Leader" Kim Il Sung, the son almost never speaks in public. In 1997, however, a high-level defector smuggled out a copy of a private speech Kim had given to party members. In it, he was critical of peddlers who sprang up on street corners to sell food during this troubled period: "This creates egotism among the people, and the base of the party's class may come to collapse. Then, the party will lose popular support and dissolve. This has been well illustrated by past incidents in Poland and Czechoslovakia."

The vast majority of North Korean refugees don't see themselves on an ideological trek to the West; indeed, many of them grew up on so much propaganda that they distrust South Korea and the U.S. They just want to feed themselves.

Kang wasn't sure what the future would hold for her, but the trafficker's threats and disappearance were a cause for concern. Kang went into hiding with friends of her brother. "For a while, I was sleeping wherever I could. I was moving around a lot," she says. Then, one day, three men carrying shotguns came to where she was staying—and Kang learned that she had been sold to them, unbeknownst to her brother. In rural China, men often buy their wives in what might be called a variant of the traditional shotgun marriage.

Kang's captors took her and three other North Korean women to a distant city, where two of them were quickly sold. The wife traders celebrated their success that evening, but their festivities came to an abrupt halt when police raided them in the middle of the night. The whole group was carted off for questioning, and for a while it looked as if Kang would be sent back to her homeland. Then one of the policemen bribed his chief. Now he took Kang with him, for the purpose of selling her as a wife. His first attempt failed, when Kang informed a potential groom that she would run away as soon as possible. The policeman beat her for this intransigence and issued more threats about a return to North Korea. Finally, a family matron intervened and promised to find Kang a good husband.

Kang relented, and was soon married to a man she describes as "semi-retarded." She thought it was the only course open to her. "I didn't know what else to do," she says. "It wasn't a real marriage.

North Korean refugees live in constant fear of discovery, knowing that they could spend the rest of their days as slave laborers.

We had no children, and the whole time I was trying to get back in touch with my brother." For two years, she couldn't find him. Then she learned of people who claimed to know where he was—and promised to reveal his location if only she would meet with them. She didn't trust them, however, and waited another year before contacting them again. This time, they provided her with information, after she promised to compensate them later on. What they gave her was a phone number in South Korea—her brother had made it out.

A Home in the South?

He was one of the lucky ones. Most North Korean refugees live in constant fear of discovery, knowing that they could spend the rest of their days as slave laborers. If they've associated with missionaries, human-rights activists, reporters, or South Koreans during their time in China, they are virtually guaranteed harsh treatment upon repatriation. Even those who leave northeast China and blend into the general Chinese population have trouble leaving the country; the borders to Mongolia, Thailand, and Vietnam are sealed, and the journeys of many North Korean refugees have ended within sight of these lands.

Last spring, several dozen refugees took to storming embassies and other diplomatic buildings in China, with mixed success. An incident in May at the Japanese consulate in Shenyang produced the most heartrending image to come out of the North Korean refugee experience: a two-year-old girl, wearing a pink-and-white dress and pigtails, sobs madly as two Chinese police officers wrestle her mother to the ground before the consulate gates. If the picture hadn't been taken, Kim Han Mee and her mother, Lee Seong Hee, would almost certainly be back in North Korea today, and perhaps not even alive. Today they're in South Korea, and so are about 1,200 other North Korean refugees who jumped into embassies or crossed borders in the past year—more in the last twelve months than in the previous half-century.

Kang had it easy, as these things go. Her brother sent about $10,000 to a refugee broker in China, who forged a set of documents, arranged a few bribes, and bought Kang a plane ticket to Seoul. She arrived in South Korea in June 2001.

South Korea's constitution says that North Koreans are automatically citizens, and in theory it should never turn away a North Korean seeking protection. Despite this, the country has been wary of accepting many North Koreans, worrying that Pyongyang might take advantage of its openness by sending spies and saboteurs. In the wake of the growing refugee crisis, however, South Koreans are more likely to fear the chaos and instability that would follow a political implosion north of the DMZ. Many would rather have North Korea's 600 Scud missiles pointed at them than face a new and different threat: the economic turmoil of assimilating millions of people now living in barbaric squalor. Today, defectors each receive about $28,000 to help with the transition. But there are only a few of them, and there's no pain-free way to extend such generosity to millions. The recent presidential election victory of Roh Moo Hyun, an outspoken anti-American politician who preaches détente with the North, was made possible by a younger generation of voters concerned more about their pocketbooks than about the North and its refugees.

Kang, for her part, is just glad to be somewhere else. "I know what freedom feels like here," she says.

Flying Toward New Dreams[2]

BY JEREMY GARLICK
THE KOREA HERALD, MAY 24, 2002

Some do it to escape a grim past or a humdrum present. Others do it to find a brighter future. Still others are motivated by a spirit of adventure or the prospect of getting rich quick. It is not for everybody, yet a sizeable number of people each year seek to leave their homeland and emigrate to other countries.

A total of 11,584 Koreans emigrated to foreign countries in 2001, according to the Ministry of Foreign Affairs and Trade. Of them, 49.2 percent emigrated to Canada, 39.4 percent to the United States, 7.1 percent to New Zealand, and 4.1 percent to Australia, meaning that a staggering 99.8 percent of Korean emigrants went to one of these four English-speaking nations.

In a crowded country like Korea, population density is clearly one reason for emigration. There simply is not enough space or opportunity for everybody. Visitors to Korea sometimes assume that packed streets and matchbox-sized apartments do not bother the locals as much as they bother people from more spacious countries like Canada or the United States. Yet Koreans are often no fonder of being squashed together like hens in a coop than they are.

"Life in Vancouver is simple and quiet, not crowded," says Moon Yoo-sook, a housewife who is trying to move her family to Canada. "That's why we want to go there. We want a slower, more relaxing life."

It is all too easy to assume that the urge to flee is a sign of failure or oppression. It is well known that many early settlers in the United States, for instance, were persecuted in their homelands. Applications for political asylum and refugee status are common across the world.

This is not the case with a democratic, peaceful country like modern Korea, however, and the reasons for emigration are more complex, with many of those aiming to fly being members of the educated middle class. According to the Canadian Embassy in Seoul, three-quarters of the approximately 7,600 Koreans who arrived in Canada as emigrants in 2000 were skilled professionals opting to make a fresh start.

Park Seung-shin is a good example. She and her husband both have degrees in architecture and would be in demand in many countries. But in Korea, as she explains, "It's difficult to get a job, espe-

---

cially for a woman. My dream is to design houses for people, but I may have to leave Korea to achieve it."

Age comes into the equation, as well as gender. "Korean society is so restricted, especially as you get older," complains Sung Pyong-sook, a schoolteacher. "I hope to teach in Australia. At least I'll find freedom and a new experience, if nothing else."

> *"Korean society is so restricted, especially as you get older."*—Sung Pyong-sook, a schoolteacher

Moon concurs on the issue of age. "My husband is 50 years old. He has no future in Korea. We want another chance," she says.

"People my age or older (in their 30s) thought they would work in a stable job for their entire lives until the IMF crisis hit Korea in 1997," explains Ran Seo-young, a part-time English teacher. "Then they began to feel scared that they could get laid off at any time. They're now trying to develop themselves so that they will have a choice of companies, instead of the companies having the choice to lay them off."

However, work is not the only reason for Koreans continuing to depart their native land. "My son's education is very important," Park says. "He's at a crucial age (15 years old), and I want to introduce him to a wider world."

"I'm not satisfied with the education system here," Moon adds. "It ruins the family life. Right now, my 13-year-old son comes home at midnight because I have to put him in a private institute to make up for the deficiencies in his public education. Education fees are also very high. I spend about half of my income on education. I think in Canada, this won't be necessary."

Education is an important motive for leaving Korea for a number of would-be emigrants. The Korean system is perceived as highly dysfunctional and as causing unnecessary stress for students to memorize, cram and pass exams. Parents feel forced to put their children into private institutes to ensure that they stay ahead.

A 2001 government survey showed that Korean parents of elementary and secondary school students were spending 7 billion won on private tutoring each year. In the overseas paradises, usually cited as Canada, the United States, New Zealand and Australia, it is thought that the quality of education is higher and cheaper, as well as demanding less of children's time.

Ran is one of those whose disappointment with the Korean education system verges on anger. "I often feel very resentful about the education I received at school," she comments. "This is the biggest reason I'm dissatisfied with life in Korea."

Additionally, of course, there is the ever-present question of the importance of the English language. The goal of emigrants is often to place themselves in countries where English is the primary language so that they and their children can join the elite class of fluent speakers of the global language. Once this goal is accomplished, they generally hope to return to Korea to conquer their homeland with their newly acquired proficiency.

"We'll stay in New Zealand for about 10 years," Park says. "Then we'll come back to Korea to live. My children will speak English by then, so they'll get good jobs."

Whatever the prospects for returning home victorious, the would-be emigrants seem to have few fears about their future lives overseas. One thing that does concern them, though, is what Moon refers to as "cultural adjustment." "I'm not sure my children will like suddenly being in another country, but I think they'll gradually get used to it," she says.

Ran is more concerned about leaving her nearest and dearest behind. "My mom and I are like close friends. We're always together every day. I'm not sure I can overcome being separated from her. I have to figure out a way for us to be together," she says.

Not even the difficulty of meeting rigorous entrance requirements to the various English-speaking nations seems to deter the would-be emigrants. The Canadian government lists a number of criteria for those wishing to live in the country, such as education, language ability and age. Of these, the second criterion seems to worry Koreans the most. The Canadian government has recently set a new standard of communicative English ability by adopting the British International English Language Testing System already used by Australia and New Zealand as a requirement for immigration to those countries.

"I'm worried about the exam," Park says, frowning. "It's very difficult for Koreans, especially the speaking test." Yet she is determined to continue her efforts to pass and start again.

So is Moon. "There is no family life in Korea," she says, shaking her head. "Five days a week, the family can't eat dinner together. I hope Korean society will change in the future, but that will be too late for us. We need a new life right now."

50 Years Later, Reunions Bring Joy to Koreans[3]

BY STEPHANIE STROM
THE NEW YORK TIMES, AUGUST 16, 2000

Under the watchful gaze of North Korean minders, 100 families separated for the last five decades today began the arduous process of rebuilding relationships torn apart by war.

In one heart-rending scene after another, mothers embraced children long given up for dead, brothers and sisters struggled to identify adults they knew until now only as children, wives steeled themselves to meet husbands long since wedded to other spouses, and vice versa.

"Thank you so much for being alive!" Hong Ghil Soon, 87, exclaimed as she embraced her daughter, Kim Ok Bae, who arrived this morning on the first North Korean plane to land on South Korean soil since 1950. "Thank the dear leader for taking such good care of you!"

The "dear leader" is Kim Jong Il, the North Korean leader whose surprisingly sophisticated political maneuvering underlay all the drama. Here was a South Korean mother whose daughter was effectively kidnapped by North Korean troops during the war heaping praise on the man whose father, Kim Il Sung, led those troops and founded the totalitarian state that split her family apart, and who until recently was himself seen by the world outside as a reclusive, dictatorial oddity.

The plane that brought the 100 people south today carried another 100 people north on its return trip for similar reunions. They were accompanied by some South Korean staff members, but without the mandate to monitor the reunions that the North's minders apparently had. The reunions today are the first in what South Korean officials hope will be a series of three sets of family gatherings this year.

Kim Jong Il, who met with South Korean news executives last week, told them that he intended to arrange two more reunions, in September and October. Southern officials say the planning for those gatherings is already in the works.

The meetings are part of a strategy, mapped out by Kim Jong Il and the South Korean president, Kim Dae Jung, in their historic meeting in June, to begin the process of reunifying the two countries by breaking down the barriers that divide their people.

Already North Korea has agreed to re-establish rail links between the two countries, and last week it signed an agreement with one of South Korea's biggest conglomerates to develop a permanent meeting place for separated families at Kaesong, just north of the border.

Kim Jong Il has even said he would like to find a way to allow visiting relatives to stay in each other's homes, rather than meet in convention centers and hotel rooms as they are doing now. But those taking part in these reunions clearly cared not a whit that they have become political pawns. They were simply happy to be families once again.

The vast convention hall where the meetings took place today reverberated with shouts of joy and peals of happy laughter, not to mention a fair amount of relieved sobbing, as families solved long-standing mysteries and confirmed or discarded long-held suspicions.

For five decades Moon Kyung Ja wondered what happened to her mother, who was thrown in jail for aiding the North Korean Army during the Korean War and was never seen again.

> *Those taking part in these reunions clearly cared not a whit that they have become political pawns.*

Today she got her answer from her eldest sister, Moon Yang Ok, whom she had not seen since the war and had at times presumed dead. Their mother did not die in jail, as Moon Kyung Ja feared, but instead escaped and walked to safety in North Korea with her two oldest daughters and baby son.

"Mother passed away without fulfilling her dream of seeing you," Moon Yang Ok told her sister while stroking her face. "But your brother and sister are alive."

"Oh, my God, they are alive!" Moon Kyung Ja shouted, throwing her hands in air. "My family is alive!"

Her sister hugged her hard. "Let me see you," she said. "Let me see your face. I have learned how long a day is, waiting this last week to see you."

Hopes are high that these are the first steps toward a more sweeping reconciliation, including greater economic cooperation and decreased military tension between the two countries, which are technically still at war.

But how far the current thaw will go remains to be seen. North Korea was careful to arrange an insurance policy against defections, making sure that the South Koreans who have gone north will not leave until all of the North Korean family members are home.

And a South Korean official said today that his country fully expected to pay the impoverished North for these reunions. Already, the South Korean government has given each family $500 to give to its visiting relatives from the North.

The North Koreans who arrived today all appear to be members of the country's elite: professors, doctors, artists and the like. During interviews a few mentioned that they had been "chosen by the dear leader" to make the trip, suggesting that they have ties to the North Korean political hierarchy.

They were in high spirits, waving and clapping as they left the plane, and seemed more affluent than their South Korean relatives had expected. Many South Koreans had bought watches to give their relatives, but many of the visitors arrived wearing nice watches. Two or three of the seven North Korean women wore exquisite—and expensive—*han dok*, traditional Korean dresses.

Nonetheless, some of the delegation's spit and polish seemed a bit contrived. Several men seemed to be wearing identical suits and identical ties, and none of them carried any hand luggage on the plane, in stark contrast to the South Koreans who went north nearly staggering under tote bags jammed with gifts.

Questions about what the visitors from the North thought of Seoul were ignored or brushed aside, and the visitors took every opportunity to praise the dear leader and the great leader, as Kim Il Sung, the founder of North Korea, was known.

Moon Yang Ok proudly showed her sister a handsome watch with "Kim Il Sung" written in elegant red calligraphy across its light silver face. "I received this as an award for my academic achievements from the great leader," she said proudly.

She teaches medicine, as does their younger brother, who was 2 when they fled for the North. "Thanks to our great leader, we have become medical professionals and my younger brother is the leading academic at the Hamheung University School of Medicine," she said. "There aren't many people like that."

She said her brother had invented a machine to treat arteriosclerosis.

But others were more unsettled by the attention they received today. "My sister seems really nervous," said Kim Suk Bae, whose sister, Kim Ok Bae, arrived in Seoul today. "Whenever the men from the other side come by, the ones with badges, she keeps praising the dear leader and tells us to do the same. We feel like we have to play along, because if we don't, something bad might happen to her when she returns to her home."

Kim Ok Bae turned her head away whenever she was asked a question, so her sister answered for her. She said Kim Ok Bae left their house in September 1950 on a school trip to perform for North Korean troops. The performance was so good that the North Koreans "recruited" the performers to travel around and keep morale high.

After the war, Kim Ok Bae became an anatomy professor, her sister said. She is married to another anatomy professor and has two children, a son who is a movie producer and a daughter who is a teacher.

Her sister said Kim Ok Bae had told the family that every year on her mother's birthday, she prepared a birthday feast, set a beautiful table and celebrated by herself. "I have lived until now with the guilt of having been a bad daughter," Kim Ok Bae said to her mother, Hong Ghil Soon, who is 87, when they met today.

"But you've turned out wonderfully!" her mother exclaimed.

Indeed, in many cases the North Korean visitors seemed better off than their southern relatives, which is probably precisely the message Kim Jong Il wished to send. Kim Hyun Ki remembered his older brother, Kim Hyun Suk, who disappeared from school shortly after the war started, as a bright, handsome, engaging youngster.

> *"I feel like a rich man today because I am able to see my family again."*—
> **Kim Dong Jin**

Today, Kim Hyun Suk did indeed seem to be all of those things—and much younger than his two younger brothers. A tall man with a thick head of salt-and-pepper hair, he spoke animatedly during their meeting.

"I went into the army for three years, and after that I went to college," he said. "They sent me to college to study engineering, and I studied really hard, father."

He said his three children also had college degrees. No one in his South Korean family, which found it difficult to scratch out a living here once the authorities found out they had a family in the North, can make a similar statement.

Kim Dong Man was not about to let his brother Kim Dong Jin forget the hard times his ideological beliefs had brought upon his family. Kim Dong Jin joined the North Korean Army after being jailed several times for his Communist beliefs.

The South Korean Army then threw his father into prison because of his son's activities and confiscated all of the family's possessions, Kim Dong Man said. "My father died because of my older brother," he said.

Kim Dong Jin, a retired civil servant, sat silently as his brother described the family's woes. "He still hasn't told me what he did for a living in the North," Kim Dong Man said. "But he did say he lives in a 100-square-yard house, and from that I know he's wealthy."

Kim Dong Jin then broke his silence. "I feel like a rich man today because I am able to see my family again," he said quietly. "But if I would have stayed in the south, I would have died.

"When I was 24 and the North Koreans took me in, all I had were my two fists. But the great leader educated me and gave me a job."

For his part, Kim Dong Man says he holds no grudges against his brother. "Older brother told me he is sorry," he said. "These tragedies happened because we lost our country to the Japanese and then fought ourselves after that. My brother was part of that. I want all of this suffering to end with my generation."

International Support a Key to Korean Peace[4]

BY JEONG SE-HYUN
KOREA.NET, JUNE 7, 2002

The Sunshine Policy is a policy for peace. It promotes peace, reconciliation, and cooperation between North and South Korea through the expansion of inter-Korean dialogue and exchange in the spirit of mutual respect. At the current stage, the policy focuses on realizing coexistence and co-prosperity between the two Koreas rather than striving for national unification.

To achieve such goals, the South Korean government has established the following three principles in its policy toward the North: first, it will not allow any form of armed provocation that will destroy peace on the Korean peninsula; second, it will attempt neither to harm nor to absorb the North; and third, it will actively promote reconciliation and cooperation between the two Koreas starting from those areas where they can be readily achieved.

While preserving peace through a strong security posture, the Sunshine Policy aims at creating an environment conducive to inducing North Korea to willingly move toward expanding dialogue and cooperation with the South as well as opening itself to the outside world.

In other words, the Sunshine Policy is a peace-keeping as well as a peace-making policy.

Keeping peace may be possible through maintaining strong defense, but strong defense alone does not guarantee peace. Mutual mistrust and fear cause an arms race and a heightened arms race further builds up mistrust and anxiety. The vicious circle continues.

That was the reason why we developed a sure way to build peace. There are two factors needed to bring about peace: the efforts of the Korean people and the support of the international community.

First, North and South Korea should reconcile with each other through expanded dialogue based on mutual respect and cross recognition. While promoting exchanges and cooperation in various areas, the South will provide assistance to help the North overcome the food crisis. Through such a process, the two Koreas will be able to thaw away hostilities formed between them throughout the era of Cold War. The removal of hostilities will become a basis from which the two Koreas can alleviate military tension between

---

4. Article by Jeong Se-hyun from *Korea.net* June 7, 2002. Copyright © *Korea.net*. Reprinted with permission.

them and achieve arms control. Furthermore, this may act as energy for political integration. Europe's process of integration aimed at the creation of the European Union through the formation of the European Economic Community has been a good reference for the Sunshine Policy.

Second, South Korea will help North Korea to participate in the international community and induce the North to join international efforts to promote peace and economic prosperity.

To achieve this, however, we need the support of our allies. We must try together to persuade North Korea to improve its relations with the United States, Japan, and the members of the European Union. We should also help the secluded country join various international economic institutions so that it becomes eligible for assistance needed in rebuilding its economy. Along with such efforts, we should also persuade the Pyongyang regime to eliminate the elements of security threat that have fed the international commu-

---

We are pursuing peace rather than war as well as cooperation rather than conflict between the two Koreas.

---

nity's concern over the communist regime and to take steps toward opening the country to the outside world.

Through the promotion of the Sunshine Policy, we are pursuing peace rather than war as well as cooperation rather than conflict between the two Koreas. We are also supporting its participation in the international community.

South Korea's Efforts Toward Peace

Since its inauguration in February 1998, the Kim Dae-jung administration has consistently promoted dialogue, exchange, and cooperation between the two Koreas and provided a large sum of assistance to the North.

During this period, the administration has taken decisive measures against any North Korean provocation while persuading domestic critics to promote expanded contact, dialogue, and cooperation with the North.

Inter-Korean dialogue and cooperation is the only way to show North Korea, which has maintained a totally closed system for more than half a century, the current times and the changed world. By doing so, we can provide an environment conducive for North Koreans to start a self-initiated reform. As mutual interdependence increases between the two Koreas, we can also improve an environment for genuine peace on the peninsula.

A substantial improvement in inter-Korean cooperation through expanded economic cooperation and humanitarian assistance has become a basis on which the two Koreas could move toward political reconciliation.

As a result, a meeting between the heads of the two Korean states took place in June 2000. This was a critical turning point, marking a new milestone in inter-Korean relations.

During the summit meeting, the two Korean leaders shared common convictions that the two Koreas must avoid war between them and dialogue and that expanding mutual cooperation is the only way to facilitate the process of national unification. Based on such agreements, the two leaders announced a joint declaration on June 15.

The June 15 Inter-Korean Joint Declaration is an agreement to expand reconciliation and cooperation and promote peaceful coexistence between the two Koreas. This was a promise between the two leaders to resolve the pending issues hanging between the two Koreas through the means of dialogue and mutual cooperation.

With the June 2000 summit, dialogue between the two Koreas flourished at various levels. Over the past couple of years, the two Koreas have discussed a wide range of bilateral issues through more than 20 rounds of talks in various areas, including six rounds of ministerial talks, defense ministers' talks, working-level military talks, meetings of joint economic promotion committee, Red Cross talks, and Mt. Kumgang tourism talks.

In September 2000, during the first defense ministers' talks to take place ever since the division of the country, both sides agreed to cooperate actively with each other to resolve military issues accompanying the implementation of the June 15 Joint Declaration. The two sides also agreed to make joint efforts to remove the threat of war. The five rounds of working-level talks subsequently held prepared ground for building military confidence between the two Koreas.

In early April this year, South Korea dispatched a presidential envoy to the North. The mission of the envoy was to prevent in advance possible circumstances that may threaten peace on the Korean peninsula in the midst of escalating tension between North Korea and the United States. Having made North Korea's supreme leader agree on resuming dialogue with Washington, the envoy contributed greatly to creating a peaceful mood on the peninsula.

In accordance with agreements made between the two governments, North and South Korea enthusiastically promoted economic cooperation and exchange. The two Koreas agreed to promote a number of joint projects, including the connection of railroads between Seoul and Shinuiju and the tracks and roads along the east coast, linkage of Trans-Siberian Railroad and Trans-Korean Railroad, development of the Kaesong industrial park, and the connection of a natural gas pipeline.

However, all these projects require the passage through the Military Demarcation Line, an area where the two Koreas' armies are sharply confronting each other, and a peaceful use of the Demilitarized Zone.

Consequently, trust and cooperation between the two military authorities are absolutely necessary to turn any of these projects into a success. These projects are ones to be promoted on the premise that peace will be established between the two Koreas in advance. In fact, inter-Korean economic cooperation facilitates military confidence building between the two Koreas.

In the Korean circumstances, not only do the measures to build military confidence contribute greatly to expanding peace on the Korean peninsula, but so do other efforts such as political reconciliation, economic cooperation, and social and cultural exchanges.

Dismantling Cold War Regime

The key to resolving the Korean problem lies obviously in improving inter-Korean relations. However, the Korean problem has a dual nature of being a national as well as an international issue.

A series of events, including the North Korean nuclear crisis in the early 1990s, controversy over the Kumchang-ri underground facilities in 1998, and test firing of Taepodong I missile, are historical facts that prove that the Korean problem can hardly be resolved independently from the international community.

Because of such peculiarities in the Korean problem, the South Korean government is determined to dismantle the Cold War structure that has become the root of various inter-Korean issues.

In other words, the government is convinced that the inter-Korean issues can be resolved only by tackling both pending and fundamental issues simultaneously. The fundamental issues refer to those related to the Cold War structure, that is, mutual mistrust and permanent threat built up among North and South Korea and the surrounding countries throughout the Cold War era.

For this reason, the dismantlement of the Cold War structure is possible only through the reduction of mutual threat and creation of mutually beneficial relations among the concerned countries. The South Korean government has taken a consistent, comprehensive, and gradual approach to achieve this goal. First, the government has promoted the Sunshine Policy with consistency. Second, it has taken a comprehensive approach. This approach calls for North and South Korea and other concerned countries such as the United States and Japan working together to negotiate political, diplomatic, economic, trade, and various other issues at once.

Third, the government has taken a gradual approach. Since dismantling the Cold War structure is a long-term process, the government has listed its priorities and tried to cope first with the issues that can be readily implemented based on a principle of give-what-we-can-and-take-what-we-should.

Fourth, the government has promoted its efforts through close cooperation with the United States and Japan while winning the support of China and Russia.

Role of International Community

South Korea will continue to promote the Sunshine Policy in the future. Just like West Germany's ostpolitik, which finally brought about German unification after 20 years of implementation, the Sunshine Policy will gradually bear its fruits years from now.

At the present stage, the Korean problem is directly related to many critical global issues such as non-proliferation of weapons of mass destruction, international solidarity against terrorism, and global security. North Korea's food shortage has also emerged as a major international issue.

To resolve these issues peacefully, the government thinks that it is important to maintain close cooperation with the international community and create a favorable environment for North Korea to improve its relations with the outside world.

Fortunately, it is encouraging to see that North Korea has recently expanded its participation in the international community and cautiously taken steps toward direction of self-reform.

North Korea has established diplomatic ties anew with 19 Western countries since the inter-Korean summit. The country also joined various international organizations, including the ASEAN Regional Forum. It has sent a number of its experts abroad to study market economy. By reinforcing its relations with China, Russia, Southeast Asian countries, and the European Union, Pyongyang has strived to improve its relations with the international community.

Considering the rigidity and peculiarity of the North Korean regime, we think that these signs of change have implications of considerable importance. For this reason, South Korea, as well as the international community, should actively encourage and support North Korea's move toward such a direction.

While making our best efforts, we are expecting an active support and cooperation of the international community to fulfill our epochal mission to open an era of peace and cooperation on the Korean peninsula.

Detente Could Unsettle
Balance of Power[5]

BY WILLIAM DAWKINS
FINANCIAL TIMES, OCTOBER 19, 2000

Neighbours and allies are nervously crossing fingers in the hope that detente between North and South Korea will render the balance of power in Asia more stable.

The official wisdom is that the rapid increase in contacts following the first summit of the two heads of state in June is to be welcomed. If all goes well, this might be the first step towards peaceful co-existence between two nations that have spent the past more than half century at loggerheads with 1.7m troops from both sides glaring at each other across east Asia's most dangerous border. But official optimism is tempered by a sense that detente will not be easy and that important questions over how all this could change the regional balance of power remain unresolved.

The uncertainties are: how far detente will really go; and whether closer relations might cause a more confident South Korea to reassess loyalties and alliances with Asia's main powers—China, Japan and the U.S.

On the first question, detente, South Korean President Kim Dae-jung is officially committed to full unification. It is his Holy Grail. But despite the genuineness of Mr. Kim's commitment to what he hopes will be his mark on history, few Korean or Western foreign policy experts in Seoul expect unification to happen for at least several years.

Why not? Close examination shows that the will for unification is weak in the ranks in South Korea and at the top in the North. In the South, the populace is worried that the government can ill afford to provide the very substantial financial aid needed to modernise North Korea's almost mediaeval economy. That worry has intensified in recent months as the decline in the Seoul stock market has reminded the electorate that the South's financial problems are a long way from being resolved. How can the South afford to bail out its impoverished neighbours?

A recent survey by the government's unification ministry showed that 60 percent of respondents believed that rapprochement with the North was going too fast. Mr. Kim, it is felt, is giving away too much too quickly.

---

5. Article by William Dawkins from *Financial Times* October 19, 2000. Copyright © *Financial Times*. Reprinted with permission.

It is hard to guess what the North really wants out of this, beyond food and economic aid to help an impoverished population. But academics in Seoul, who specialise in divining what lies in North Korean leader Kim Jong-Il's mind, assume that the northern rapprochement is constrained by fear of domination by the South. Hence, a revealing debate between the two Kims over whether a unified Korea should be a federation with a single government; or a con federation of two independent states.

South Korean foreign policy academics assume that a controlled and partial opening is Kim Jong-Il's objective. He sees no interest in frustrating Kim Dae-jung by pulling unification off the agenda, but neither does Kim Jong-Il have an interest in pursuing it too hard. "Kim Jong-Il is seeking a balance between opening up and still keeping the population insulated from infection from outside," says a senior diplomat.

If detente looks as if it will be gradual, this will probably suit the two Koreas' neighbours. Peaceful relations between North and South would be in the common interest of China, Japan and the

---

"Kim Jong-Il is seeking a balance between opening up and still keeping the population insulated from infection from outside."—a senior diplomat

---

U.S. But if the Koreas were to move from normalisation on to seek unification, then the interests of their neighbours start to diverge.

There is much speculation among politicians in Seoul, for instance, over whether a unified Korea might swing closer into China's orbit. That would mark a very important change from South Korea's traditional post–Korean war position as a balancing power in the struggle for supremacy between China and Japan.

Unification might also weaken South Korean support for the U.S. to continue to keep its troops in the country. Currently, their presence is welcomed across the region from Taipei to Tokyo for keeping the lid on any temptation China might feel to go expansionist, just as they are welcomed in China and Pyongyang for keeping a lid on Japan.

Even North Korea, which has long opposed the presence of U.S. troops in South Korea, has recently switched its position to accepting them, even after unification.

"Many Koreans—both north and south—fear that their country will swing into the Chinese orbit after unification, and the continued presence of U.S. troops will prevent that," says a diplomat in Seoul.

The prospect of a hard-to-handle unified Korea is, for now, remote. Diplomats are bargaining that relations between North and South will simply inch closer. Reduced tension is likely to make the South more confident, though not necessarily more assertive, in its foreign relations. If that turns out to be the case, the regional balance will not change much.

The U.S., whatever the outcome of the presidential election, will have a continued interest in keeping troops in the South to underwrite regional security. It can expect a continued official welcome from the South, even if it is marred by the occasional local gripes about the nuisance caused by military exercises.

Detente with the North has already weakened the public's tolerance of U.S. troops. And yet the U.S. military alliance remains of deep importance to the South Korean government—and to all the main political parties. The Korean establishment's pro–U.S. consensus is very like Japan's consensus for its U.S. military links. Both countries' defenses are underwritten by Washington, and both countries' governments experience occasional domestic criticism for their pro–U.S. policies.

The view from Washington is that U.S. troops continue to play a vital role. Despite the new rapprochement between Seoul and Pyongyang, policy makers do not believe that the last remaining front in the Cold War is anywhere near falling. It remains, as a visiting President Bill Clinton once observed, the scariest place on earth.

A Small Problem Growing[6]

BY BARBARA DEMICK
LOS ANGELES TIMES, FEBRUARY 12, 2004

At 16, Myung Bok is old enough to join the North Korean army. But you wouldn't believe it from his appearance. The teenager stands 4 feet 7, about the size of an American sixth-grader.

Myung Bok escaped the communist North last summer to join his mother and younger sisters, who had fled to China earlier. When he arrived, 14-year-old sister Eun Hang didn't recognize the scrawny little kid walking up the dirt path to their cottage in a village near the North Korean border. She hadn't seen him in four years.

"He's short. I can't believe he used to be my big brother," Eun Hang said sadly as she recalled their early childhood, when Myung Bok was always a full head taller. Now she can peek over the crown of his head without standing on her tiptoes.

The teenagers go through an almost daily ritual: They stand against a wooden wardrobe in which they've carved notches with a penknife, hoping that by eating a regular diet Myung Bok will grow tall enough to reclaim his status as big brother.

They're not the only ones obsessed with height. The short stature of North Koreans reflects an international humanitarian crisis—one fraught with diplomatic and political overtones. It is at the heart of a debate in the international community over whether North Korea should continue to get food aid despite its quest for nuclear weapons.

The World Food Program and UNICEF reported last year that chronic malnutrition had left 42 percent of North Korean children stunted—meaning their growth was seriously impaired, most likely permanently. An earlier report by the United Nations agencies warned that there was strong evidence that physical stunting could be accompanied by intellectual impairment.

South Korean anthropologists who measured North Korean refugees here in Yanji, a city 15 miles from the North Korean border, found that most of the teenage boys stood less than 5 feet tall and weighed less than 100 pounds. In contrast, the average 17-year-old South Korean boy is 5-foot-8, slightly shorter than an American boy of the same age.

The height disparities are stunning because Koreans were more or less the same size—if anything, people in the North were slightly taller—until the abrupt partitioning of the country after

World War II. South Koreans, feasting on an increasingly West-ern-influenced diet, have been growing taller as their estranged countrymen have been shrinking through successive famines.

It is brutal proof of the old aphorism: You are what you eat.

"Human beings are really plastic. Features and size are not entirely racial, but are greatly affected by diet," said Chung Byong Ho, a South Korean anthropologist who worked on the Yanji study, which was published in December in the academic publication *Korea Journal.* "We Koreans are genetically homogenous, but we are not really the same anymore."

Foreigners who get the chance to visit North Korea—perhaps the most isolated country in the world—are often confused about the age of children. Nine-year-olds are mistaken for kindergartners and soldiers for Boy Scouts.

"They all looked like dwarfs," said Kim Dong Kyu, a South Korean academic who has made two trips to North Korea. "When I saw those soldiers, they looked like middle school students. I thought if they had to sling an M-1 rifle over their shoulders, it would drag to the ground."

"When I saw those soldiers, they looked like middle school students. I thought if they had to sling an M-1 rifle over their shoulders, it would drag to the ground."—
Kim Dong Kyu, South Korean academic

To the extent that they ever get to meet South Koreans, the North Koreans are likewise shocked. When two diminutive North Korean soldiers, ages 19 and 23, accidentally drifted into South Korea on a boat, one reportedly was overheard saying they would never be able to marry South Korean women because they were "too big for us," according to an account in the book "The Two Koreas," by Don Oberdorfer. The soldiers were repatriated to the North at their own request.

The North Koreans appear to be sensitive about their stature. In dealings with the outside world, the country likes to present a tall image by sending statuesque (by North Korean standards) athletes to joint sporting events in South Korea and elsewhere and assigning the tallest soldiers to patrol at the demilitarized zone that divides the countries.

Starting in the mid-1990s, North Korean leader Kim Jong Il (who reportedly wears elevator shoes to boost his 5-foot-3 height) ordered people to do special exercises designed to make them taller. As a result, it is not uncommon to see students hanging from rings or parallel bars for as long as 30 minutes. Basketball is also promoted as a national sport to instill the yearning for height.

"Grow taller!" instruct banners hung in some schoolyards, defectors and aid workers say.

Seok Young Hwan, a North Korean army doctor who defected to South Korea in 1998, said the Health Ministry also ordered government research institutes to investigate herbal remedies and vitamins believed to promote growth. One popular Chinese medicine distributed to soldiers and students is made of pine tree powder, another of calcium.

"People are really fixated on what they need to do to make children grow," Seok said.

It appears that none of these curatives has been effective— although North Korea can boast of the world's tallest basketball player, 7-foot-9 Li Myung Hoon, who is believed to have a pituitary imbalance. The North Korean military had so much difficulty finding tall enough recruits that it had to revoke its minimum height requirement of 5-foot-3. Many soldiers today are less than 5 feet tall, defectors say.

Height, however, is only the outward manifestation of the problem. The more troublesome aspect of stunting is the effect on health, stamina and intelligence.

"There is a difference between being naturally small because your parents are small. That's not a problem," Seok said. "But if you're small because you weren't able to eat as a child, you are bound to be less intelligent."

The issue of IQ is sufficiently sensitive that the South Korean anthropologists studying refugee children in China have almost entirely avoided mentioning it in their published work in *Korea Journal*. But they say it is a major unspoken worry for South Koreans, who fear that they could inherit the burden of a seriously impaired generation if the Koreas are reunified.

"This is our nightmare," anthropologist Chung said. "We don't want to get into racial stereotyping or stigmatize North Koreans in any way. But we also worry about what happens if we are living together and we have this generation that was not well fed and well educated."

About 500 North Korean children have come to South Korea, either alone or with their parents, and they are known to have difficulty keeping up in the school system, say people who work with defectors.

Although South Korea gives defectors priority in going to the best universities in a form of affirmative action, about 80 percent have dropped out, Chung said.

"People assume that children are more adaptive than adults, but it is not always so. Famine is not just malnutrition, but often a long period in which education is disrupted," Chung said. "South Korea is education hell. It is very competitive, and there is no way for them to catch up."

Pak Sun Young, an anthropologist at Seoul National University who measured the children in China, said the height disparity alone would subject North Koreans to discrimination. "In almost every society, taller-than-average people are preferred. Short people have a harder time getting a job," Pak said. "People already talk about how short North Koreans are. We are a very looks-conscious society."

From an anthropological standpoint, the North Korea situation has attracted interest because it is, Pak said, the first documented case in which a homogeneous group of people has become so distinct because of nutrition and lifestyle.

Because North Korea is so secretive about statistics, it is difficult to quantify the height disparity between North and South. The anthropologists who worked in China caution that the 55 refugee children they measured are probably smaller than the children of elite party cadres in Pyongyang, the capital, who are better fed.

"I just can't respect anybody that would really let his people starve and shrink in size as a result of malnutrition."— **President George W. Bush**

There is virtually no height difference among adults older than 40, who came of age at a time when the North's economy was on a par with that of the South. The trouble is most acute with those younger than 20, who were in peak growth years during the mid-1990s, when North Korea experienced a famine that is believed to have killed 2 million people—10 percent of the population.

Like almost everything else to do with North Korea, discussions of height are deeply wrapped up in politics. Conservatives—in South Korea and the United States, among others—who may prefer a change in leadership in North Korea point to residents' shrinking stature as evidence of Kim's failure.

"I just can't respect anybody that would really let his people starve and shrink in size as a result of malnutrition," President Bush told White House reporters in October.

Humanitarian agencies argue that more food aid is needed for North Korea to prevent the stunting of more children. North Korea's pursuit of nuclear weapons has made the country unpopular with donors, who are faced with competing crises in Iraq and Afghanistan.

The World Food Program said this week that it had secured less than one-third of the 485,000 tons of food needed for North Korea this year and that it had been forced to cut off almost all its 6.5 million food aid recipients until April. Although more food is available at private markets because of economic reforms, the U.N. agency said, the prices are out of reach for most North Koreans.

Emergency intervention after the famine of the mid-1990s brought about a dramatic improvement, but the situation could rapidly reverse itself, experts warn.

"We've gone from seeing six out of 10 children to four out of 10 children stunted, but that is still, medically speaking, a crisis, and the gains are not irreversible," said Masood Hyder, the U.N.'s humanitarian coordinator in Pyongyang.

Another aspect of the problem is that children stunted through malnutrition can be permanently impaired even if the food supply improves.

Myung Bok, for example, comes from Chongjin on North Korea's east coast, which was hit particularly hard by the famine.

Even afterward, the food supply was meager. Until he left in August, the teenager ate mostly corn porridge mixed with rice and an occasional cabbage leaf. He and his grandmother hunted for wild herbs and plants to supplement their diet.

"We had meat maybe once or twice a year for special occasions, like Kim Jong Il's birthday," said Myung Bok, a quiet boy who, for lack of other clothes, wears his sister's pink stretch pants and a spangled sweater. "We never had milk that I can remember."

Even by the standards of rural China, the family is poor. But they manage to eat rice and vegetables every day, meat three or four times a week. Fourteen-year-old Eun Hang has virtually caught up with other children her age since leaving North Korea when she was 10.

The prognosis for Myung Bok—and millions like him still in North Korea—is less certain.

"There is catch-up growth in children who are malnourished. Boys can grow up to age 22, but they have to have access to good diet and healthcare," said Judit Katona-Apte, a nutritionist with the World Food Program who is working on stunting issues in North Korea.

Anthropologist Pak was less encouraging.

"For North Korea as a whole, the situation could change in a generation. The people are genetically identical to us," she said. "But for the individuals who are already short, there isn't much to do. Usually by the time you are in your late teens, more calories won't make you taller, only fatter."

III. Foreign Relations

Editor's Introduction

Since the end of the Cold War and the collapse of the Soviet Union, North Korea has found itself without the political, financial, and military support it once enjoyed. Once a key communist player backed by the Soviet Union and China, North Korea is today viewed by the international community as a rogue nation lacking direction. Its economy has been driven into the ground by policies focused primarily on the military, and its people are poor and starving. Foreign aid has become the only way for North Korea to keep its head above water, forcing it to attempt diplomatic relations with other countries—namely Japan and China. South Korea, on the other hand, has openly pursued relations with other countries for several years. While the U.S. military is still actively involved in South Korea's defense, the country forms international ties not out of necessity, like its northern neighbor, but out of a desire to be more involved in the global community. Chapter three examines both North and South Korea's foreign policies with an emphasis on U.S.–South Korean relations in light of the U.S. presence at the DMZ.

The first article in this chapter looks at North Korea's dealings with Japan. While the Japanese provide a large amount of aid to the North Koreans, Japan is wary of trade between their two countries. In "Japan Shrugs off North Korean Threats over Inspections," Mark Magnier discusses Japanese concerns. Because so many commonplace items can be reused or broken down to make or transport nuclear weapons and other types of armaments, the Japanese are taking every precaution not to ship anything to North Korea that could potentially be used for militarization. In his article, Magnier examines the different uses of everyday items in defense-related projects, and addresses North Korea's threat to cease diplomatic relations with Japan altogether unless the latter country loosens its maritime restrictions against it.

As South Korea has opened its doors to foreign relations, it has let in a once unlikely partner: China. A staunch supporter of North Korea under Mao Zedong, China has recently begun to view South Korea as more friend than foe. And while South Koreans still think of China as "the big brother," they are also beginning to see China as the main Asian powerhouse, and therefore a good ally to have on their side. "Courtship of Beijing and Seoul: A New Twist for an Old Bond" by James Brooke describes the new wave of "China-mania" that has swept South Korea, as well as the exchanges that are taking place between the two countries.

In addition to opening their doors to China, South Koreans are also beginning to deal with Japan, a country that has severely oppressed them in the past. Although each still has a good deal of animosity toward the other lurking just below the surface, Korea and Japan are conducting many cultural, economic, and educational exchanges. "Long Indifferent, Japanese Are Drawn to South Korea," written by Norimitsu Onishi, discusses the new wave of friendly relations between these former antagonists. Onishi explains how South Koreans are separating history from culture in order to foster and perpetuate these newfound feelings of goodwill, which were strengthened by the 2002 World Cup co-hosted by South Korea and Japan. An accompanying sidebar provides an overview of South Korea's foreign relations policies since the Korean War.

The remaining articles in the chapter focus on the American presence within South Korea and the rise of anti-Americanism among the younger generation of South Koreans. In his article "Honor Guard," Eric Weiner discusses recent events that have triggered a wave of anti-Americanism among South Koreans. He also briefly touches upon the arrangements that have been made to begin moving American troops out of the South Korean capital of Seoul in response to the backlash against the American presence. "S. Korean President: Nothing to Worry About Relocation of U.S. Troops from Seoul," from The Associated Press, provides an overview of domestic issues surrounding the U.S. presence in South Korea and future plans for American troops on the peninsula, as well as an in-depth discussion of the decision to remove 7,000 American troops and their families from Seoul—perhaps the first step toward a complete American troop withdrawal.

The debate over an American presence in South Korea is fueled by two divergent views among the South's populace. One view, held by the older generation, who remember the Korean War, supports an American presence. The second view, held by the younger generation, scorns American military aid. This difference in attitudes is the subject of Michael Dorgan's article "S. Korea's Divisions." While the younger generation views the North as "brothers" and the Americans as intruders who have overstayed their welcome, the older generation has memories of a bloody war waged against their families by those so-called "brothers" and views the Americans as saviors who are still protecting them against a North Korean insurgence. Dorgan discusses this generational gap in attitudes and the circumstances surrounding current thinking.

Japan Shrugs off N. Korean Threats over Inspections[1]

By Mark Magnier
Los Angeles Times, June 13, 2003

Japan on Thursday brushed off threats by Pyongyang that it would torpedo relations between the two countries unless Tokyo eased up on maritime restrictions against North Korean vessels.

"We have conducted such inspections in line with our law," Chief Cabinet Secretary Yasuo Fukuda told reporters, adding that he hoped North Korea would judge Japan's newly tightened inspection procedures against the communist state in a "reasonable and cool-headed manner."

North Korea suspended the only ferry service to Japan this week in response to the tough talk from Tokyo on ship inspections. Japanese officials say the crackdown is needed in part to prevent shipment of consumer goods that could be converted to military hardware. These include everything from high-end Japanese golf clubs—extracted titanium carbon fibers are used in missile housings—to off-the-shelf global positioning system hardware capable of steering missiles; to electronic fish finders that can be converted to sonar devices.

Even the lenses of store surveillance cameras can find a second life as submarine periscopes, experts said, and something as mundane as high-quality shampoo can be filtered for its triethanolamine and used in making chemical weapons.

"Any time they order huge amounts of anything, or buy expensive things, that should make us suspicious," said Shigeharu Aoyama, director of Japan's Independent Institute, a think tank based in Tokyo. "There are a lot of difficult judgment calls."

While many of these items are widely available around the world, Japan's close geographic proximity, the ferry service between the two nations and a sizable population in Japan with ancestral ties to North Korea means that Japan is Pyongyang's shopping center of choice.

Japan—which has various export-control laws and protocols in place, including a version of the 1991 U.S. "catch-all" Enhanced Proliferation Control Initiative it passed in 2002—has neither the inclination nor the time to block shampoo shipments. But it does have more authority to stop some sophisticated dual-use items.

Exports of more than two Sony PlayStation 2 video game players, for instance, are subject to Japanese export licenses, given their potential use in missile guidance systems. Also subject to review are airtight beer fermentation tanks of over 100 liters, given their potential use in incubating large quantities of biological hazards.

Japan's trade ministry said that it turned down a request from several Japanese-based trading companies who had sought permission between December and March to export 30-ton tractor-trailers to North Korea. North Korea is woefully short of large vehicles capable of transporting mid-range ballistic missiles.

In reality, however, analysts say it's a pretty leaky barrier. "It's impossible to stop everything," said Hideya Kurata, a professor of nuclear security at Tokyo's Kyorin University. "A lot of this is just a big performance by the Japanese government."

Other seemingly everyday items in an advanced economy that officials here say they're worried about include freeze-drying equipment used by instant-food manufacturers, which might have a second life in biochemical weapons production, and hydrogen fluoride, which could be of use in processing uranium.

"We all know suspicious goods are being sent to North Korea, and we try and check thoroughly whenever necessary."—Satoshi Shimono, Osaka customs office

---

"We all know suspicious goods are being sent to North Korea, and we try and check thoroughly whenever necessary," said Satoshi Shimono, an official with the Osaka customs office. "We have a list of export control items, but the list is secret, so no one can know exactly what we're looking for. But it can be a difficult task given that even used aluminum tire rims can supposedly be extracted to form parts of warheads."

Toshio Miyatsuka, an expert on North Korea at Yamanashi Gakuin University, said Pyongyang also scoops up used tires for fuel and old refrigerators containing chlorofluorocarbons, which it extracts to wash computer chips. And it fills ships returning to North Korea with huge numbers of used bicycles, he added, that it buys cheaply from local governments via intermediaries after they're abandoned outside rail stations. Once back in North Korea, the ball bearings are extracted for military use, Miyatsuka said.

Last month, a North Korean defector testified before U.S. Congress that 90 percent of the components used in Pyongyang's missile program came through the now suspended ferry service. Japanese were further jarred when a North Korean spy ship recently salvaged from the seabed off Japan turned up brimming with Japanese technology.

But Wednesday at the Japan seaport of Maizuru, where a North Korean vessel was briefly detained for safety infractions, a local official said it was business as usual.

"I heard [Japanese Transport Minister Chikage Ogi] declare we were going to tighten up the system, but we haven't heard anything from our bosses about it," said Masami Nakamori, an official with the Maizuru safety inspection bureau. "We're just doing ordinary port patrols, nothing more."

In its commentary following Japan's announcement, Pyongyang slammed Japan for suggesting that its ferry was transporting spies and nuclear and missile-related parts. "This damages the great authority and image of our homeland," the state news agency said.

Meanwhile, on Thursday, Japanese police arrested five executives of Tokyo-based Seishin Enterprises on charges of illegally exporting sophisticated jet mills to Iran. The machinery can be used to help make solid rocket fuel for missiles.

Courtship of Beijing and Seoul: A New Twist for an Old Bond[2]

BY JAMES BROOKE
THE NEW YORK TIMES, FEBRUARY 26, 2004

Mao Zedong once declared that China and North Korea were "as close as lips and teeth." But as talks get under way in Beijing over North Korea's nuclear weapons program, the focus of China's affections has shifted.

While Chinese troops saved North Korea from military defeat half a century ago, the Koreans that modern Chinese identify with are in the South. K-pop music, South Korean boyfriends and tourist excursions to Seoul are all the rage in Beijing and Shanghai.

In turn, South Korea, a decade after opening diplomatic ties with China, is in the throes of China-mania. Convinced that China is Asia's power of the future, South Koreans are throwing themselves into Chinese study, travel and investment.

Today, for example, 30,000 South Koreans study in China, the largest group of foreign students there.

"When Chinese-language proficiency tests were given worldwide last year, 50 percent of the passing students were from Korea," said Zhang Jifang, the New China News Agency's bureau chief here. Near the bureau in Seoul, Beijing is building a Chinese Cultural Center, one of the largest in the world.

Six South Korean cities now have direct flights to Shanghai, while a traveler in Seoul has a choice of direct flights to 24 Chinese cities.

On the wings of this human exchange, about three million people last year, South Korea's exports to China jumped 50 percent last year, and South Korea's annual flow of investment to China hit $2.5 billion, more than triple South Korea's investment in the United States. Last year, nearly half of South Korea's foreign investment went to China.

Chasing after low labor costs and an enormous and rapidly expanding market, South Korean investors were to a great extent joining in a global flood of investment money to China, a flow that leaves some South Koreans nervous. Since 2000, the annual flow of new foreign investment into South Korea has fallen by 58 percent, hitting $6.5 billion last year.

Last year, China displaced Japan as the biggest trader in Northeast Asia, with $851 billion in regional trade. Trade between China and South Korea reached $50 billion last year, about eight times the level of a decade ago.

Historically, Koreans have viewed China as a source of culture as well as commerce, adopting Confucianism and Chinese characters, among other things. On the other hand, the relationship of vassal state to China was often oppressive.

"It is ingrained in the Korean psyche that China is the big brother," said Samuel Koo, president of Arirang TV, South Korea's English-language broadcaster. "But Chinese-Korean relations were far from being an unmitigated love affair. We used to ship to them tens of thousands of virgins every year," as a tribute hundreds of years ago.

In contrast, Japan was often seen as a violent threat, invading numerous times before the early 20th-century colonization. Aidan Foster-Carter, a Korea expert at Leeds University in Britain, calls South Korea's contemporary infatuation with China "penultimate oppressor love."

Many Koreans wonder how they will cope with a market-oriented China. Some of China's biggest investments are in areas where South Korea is currently king—shipbuilding, semiconductors, and cars.

And in what would be China's first purchase of an overseas carmaker, a state-owned conglomerate, China National Blue Star Group, is preparing to buy Ssangyong Motor, South Korea's fourth-largest car company. In addition to the purchase price, the Chinese have promised to invest $1 billion in the company. But South Korean workers seem troubled by the idea of working for a Chinese boss, and the carmaker's labor unions here have carried out half-day shutdowns in protest.

Long Indifferent, Japanese Are Drawn to South Korea[3]

By Norimitsu Onishi
The New York Times, February 22, 2004

For Yuko Fueki, a 25-year-old actress, and many other Japanese of her generation, the country next door drew a blank. But four years ago, she stumbled upon a South Korean movie that whetted her interest. It led her to study Korean and eventually to move here [South Korea], where she became South Korea's first Japanese television star.

"Until I saw that movie, I had no interest at all in Korea," said Ms. Fueki, who has also taken a Korean stage name, Yu Min. "I knew it was a nearby country, next to China. Like many people around me, I really didn't know anything at all. But things have really improved now. There's a lot more interest in Korea as a country."

In recent years, especially since Japan and South Korea were co-hosts of the World Cup in 2002, the exchange in popular culture has risen sharply. Although the legacies of Japan's brutal colonial rule here remain close to the surface, the cultural interchange signifies a profound change in the relations between the countries since Japanese troops withdrew at the end of World War II.

Last month, South Korea lifted almost all restrictions on the import of Japanese culture after tentatively opening its market in 1998. For the first time, South Koreans can legally buy CD's of Japanese singers and rent Japanese movies at the local video store. Japanese can now be heard on cable television, which until recently would have been greeted with the same kind of outraged reaction from some listeners as playing Wagner does in Israel.

In Japan, many people who had never thought about the Korean peninsula are watching South Korean television dramas and studying the language. Kimchi—the spicy pickled vegetable that is Korea's national dish—would have been dismissed a generation ago, but it is now becoming a favorite in Japan.

A new generation of entertainers like Ms. Fueki—or BoA, a Korean singer who is now famous in Japan—are effortlessly crossing borders between the countries, as well as to Taiwan, Singapore and China.

This opening of markets to Japan has occurred as South Korean confidence grows in its own "soft" power. In 1998, the same year South Korea began tentatively allowing in Japanese culture, the government put into effect its first five-year plan to build up its one culture industry.

Lee Bo Kyoung, an official in the Ministry of Culture, said the government aided specific cultural areas by providing scholarships and equipment to many schools. The number of college departments dealing with careers in culture has risen from almost none to 300 today. Cultural exports have nearly doubled since 1998—especially movies, video games and television.

The second five-year plan will focus on raising exports and building cross-cultural ties, including with Japan and China, Mr. Lee said.

Bans still remain on imports of Japanese animation and certain television programs, but they appear driven less by a need to protect culture than markets. Mr. Lee said the government agreed to restrict Japanese animation until 2006 at the request of South Korea's growing animation industry.

The sudden attraction to Korean culture and language is striking given Japan's colonial history in Korea.

Young South Koreans and Japanese are overwhelmingly the consumers of each other's culture.

"When the young people today have political power and are running our societies," Mr. Lee said, "then we will feel the full impact of this cultural exchange."

In Japan, South Korean television dramas have become so popular that organized tours bring Japanese to filming locations here. Chiyako Inoue, 43, a homemaker from Matsue, in western Japan, said she became so enthralled by one South Korean drama that she began studying Korean.

According to Japan's Ministry of Education, the number of Korean language programs in high schools was 163 in 2000, compared with 73 in 1994 and 7 in 1986. The number of private language schools that teach Korean has also mushroomed.

The sudden attraction to Korean culture and language is striking given Japan's colonial history in Korea, which it ruled from 1910 to 1945. Just as Dakar's gaze goes largely unrequited by Paris, postwar Japan chose to forget about the Koreas, fixing its attention on America.

In a cafe in a fashionable corner of Seoul, Ms. Fueki, who grew up in Tokyo, recalled that one of her friends even thought that Korea was a region in China. Until she came here and made it a point of reading books on Japanese colonial rule, Ms. Fueki herself said she had known very little about it.

"I hadn't studied it as extensively as Koreans do from the time they are schoolchildren," she said. "There are really only a few lines in our school textbooks that said, 'These are things that happened, and Koreans don't have good feelings toward Japanese.' That was the extent of it.

"If there was like or dislike, if there was some feeling, that would have been good. But there is nothing scarier than indifference. And young Japanese were indifferent toward the Koreas."

When she first appeared on television here, Ms. Fueki played a deaf-mute and—on the advice of her managers who feared she might be rejected—hid her nationality. After she revealed it, she said the reaction was evenly divided.

Since then, as the only Japanese acting regularly here, she has been put in the unusual—and sometimes uncomfortable—position of responding to political issues like how Japanese textbooks should portray the region's history and the ownership of a disputed island.

For young Koreans, consuming Japanese popular culture means separating it from Japan's history or policies.

Last year, she realized how a past that Japan would like to forget remained alive and raw here. A group of women who had been used as sex slaves by the Japanese Imperial Army invited her to visit their home. She spent the day with them, talking and cooking. But the next day a South Korean newspaper reported something she had not done.

"They wrote that I had gone there representing Japan and offered a tearful apology," she said. "I was stunned."

She was also stunned by the reaction in Japan. "Then I received a lot of e-mail in protest to my Web page, phone calls and even letters, from Japanese who still don't acknowledge those facts. That's when I learned there are still many people like that. One university professor said, 'Those things didn't happen. Why did you go and apologize?'"

For young Koreans, consuming Japanese popular culture means separating it from Japan's history or policies—the same way many people approach American culture.

Kim So Hee, 21, a college student, was buying the latest CD of the Japanese band L'Arc-en-Ciel at the J-Pop section in the Kyobo Bookstore here. She had been listening to Japanese music for five years, downloading it from the Internet, and was glad she could now buy it legally.

Still, an incident that occurred during a visit to Tokyo in December gave her pause. On Dec. 23, the birthday of the Japanese emperor, she said she stumbled upon a parade with people waving Japan's flag—a hated symbol of imperialism throughout much of Asia.

"When I saw those flags, I wanted to cover them all" with a big South Korean flag, she said. "I wondered to myself whether it was really O.K. to like this culture. Can I really separate the culture from the history? But now I've calmed down and I can separate the two."

Korea, South—Foreign Relations

Foreign Relations

In August 1991, South Korea joined the United Nations along with North Korea and has remained active in most U.N. specialized agencies and many international forums. The Republic of Korea also hosted major international events such as the 1988 Summer Olympics and the 2002 World Cup Soccer Tournament (co-hosted with Japan).

The Republic of Korea maintains diplomatic relations with more than 170 countries and a broad network of trading relationships. The United States and Korea are allied by the 1954 Mutual Defense Treaty. Korea and Japan coordinate closely on numerous issues. This includes consultations with the United States on North Korea policy.

Economic considerations have a high priority in Korean foreign policy. The ROK seeks to build on its economic accomplishments to increase its regional and global role. It is a founding member of the Asia-Pacific Economic Cooperation (APEC) forum.

Korean Peninsula: Reunification and Recent Developments

Since the Korean War, relations between North and South Korea have been strained. Official contact did not occur until in 1971, beginning with Red Cross contacts and family reunification projects. However, divergent positions on the process of reunification, North Korean weapons programs and South Korea's tumultuous domestic politics contributed to a cycle of warming and cooling of relations between North and South.

Relations improved following the 1997 election of Kim Dae-jung. His policy of 'Sunshine Policy' of engagement with North Korea set the stage for the historic June 2000 Inter-Korean summit. President Kim was awarded the Nobel Peace Prize in 2000 for the policy.

Relations have again become tense, however, following the October 2002 North Korean admission of a covert nuclear program.

Source: *www.geographyiq.com*

Honor Guard[4]

BY ERIC WEINER
THE NEW REPUBLIC, FEBRUARY 3, 2003

I had an illuminating conversation with a South Korean woman the other day. She is very worried, she explained, about a dangerous nation armed with nuclear weapons and intent on stirring up trouble. The leader of this nation, she said, won't heed the call of the international community. "Yes," I replied, "everyone is concerned about North Korea." "No, no," she replied, "not North Korea. I'm talking about the United States."

While world attention is focused on North Korea's nuclear shenanigans, another Korean crisis has erupted. One American diplomat describes it as "the most tense and difficult time" he has experienced in 33 years of dealing with South Korea. The *Chosun Ilbo*, a South Korean daily, has declared that "United States–Korea relations are at the worst point in their history." Why have relations soured so dramatically? Because many in Washington have failed to recognize that South Korea is now a world-class economic power and a robust democracy—in other words, a mature nation demanding to be treated like an equal, not the pliable client the United States often views it as.

To understand the current rift between Washington and Seoul, put down the front page of a newspaper and pick up the sports page. Look up one name in particular: Kim Dong Sung. Haven't heard of him? The South Koreans have. Kim Dong Sung is the South Korean short-track speed skater who was disqualified from the Salt Lake City Olympics for interfering with another competitor. The gold medal went to an American instead, Apolo Anton Ohno, and the South Korean public, which follows short-track speed skating obsessively, was furious. The South Korean Olympic delegation filed a protest with the International Skating Union, and Ohno received thousands of threatening e-mails from angry South Koreans.

What does speed skating have to do with the strategic alliance between the United States and South Korea? Everything. South Korea is a nation coming into its own. After decades of military rule, stable democracy has finally taken root here. South Korea bounced back from the 1997 Asian financial crisis faster and further than any other country in the region. Its economy is now humming along, growing by a brisk 6 percent per year. South Korea is the most wired nation in the world. More than half of all homes have broadband Internet access, and a recent survey by a local newspaper

---

4. Article by Eric Weiner from *The New Republic* February 3, 2003. Copyright © *The New Republic*. Reprinted with permission.

showed that 70 percent of South Koreans in their twenties and thirties surf the Internet on a daily basis. Large South Korean companies, such as Hyundai and Samsung, have become multinational conglomerates, exporting all over the world.

For South Koreans, success in speed skating and other sports serves as a vindication of their rightful place in the world. South Korea co-hosted last year's World Cup and walked away

> *South Korea and the United States view the Stalinist North through two different lenses.*

with a surprise fourth-place finish. "That was an incredibly big event for us," Douglas Shin, a Korean-American who divides his time between Washington and Seoul, told me. "Soccer here is equated with national strength, and everybody seems to believe that we are now the fourth most powerful nation in the world."

Younger South Koreans in particular exhibit this heightened nationalism. Exit polls after December's presidential election, won by Roh Moo Hyun, a former human rights lawyer who ran a campaign infused with nationalism and anti-Americanism, indicated that Roh was trailing his opponent until approximately 1 P.M., when young voters began to line up at the polls, and he then took the lead.

Koreans, in other words, are in an assertive frame of mind—in no mood to take orders from the United States. But the Olympic skating fiasco left many people here feeling that the United States still doesn't treat them with respect. And the Bush administration has compounded the resentment Koreans feel over American condescension. In March 2001, South Korean President Kim Dae Jung visited Washington, eager to convince President Bush of the wisdom of his "sunshine policy" toward the North, which called for engaging Pyongyang. Instead, Bush railed against the North as Kim Dae Jung stood silently by his side, essentially being told what to do.

President Bush's decision to include North Korea in the axis of evil further rankled South Koreans. South Korea and the United States view the Stalinist North through two different lenses. Americans see North Korea as a nation of oddballs. South Koreans also find the North Koreans weird but are hesitant to say so out loud because they have to live with them. It's the difference between someone else's crazy cousin and your crazy cousin. Kim Dae Jung's sunshine policy was especially popular with South Koreans in their twenties and thirties, men and women too young to remember the Korean War. A recent survey of South Korean high school and college students conducted by a government ministry found that 90 percent would welcome a North Korean as their next-door neighbor.

Many South Koreans see the dispute on the Korean peninsula as a family affair and the United States as the nosy outsider who keeps interfering. Yet, after the North Korean nuclear crisis erupted last October, the Bush administration did not actively seek the South's guidance. South Korean officials complain to reporters that the Bush administration plowed ahead with its North Korea strategies for months without heeding the advice of officials in Seoul, who were suggesting that Washington initiate a dialogue with Pyongyang, a view the United States now seems to have reluctantly accepted.

Part of the problem is that, despite South Korea's development into a democracy and an economic power, American policymakers are stuck with an outdated image of the South as the quaint, backward nation portrayed in the TV show *M*A*S*H*. Jeffrey Jones, former president of the American Chamber of Commerce in Korea, recalls a conversation with a U.S. representative who asked, "How are the peasants in South Korea doing?" Jones, a fluent Korean speaker, concluded that when it comes to South Korea most American officials are "ridiculously condescending and uninformed."

***American policymakers are stuck with an outdated image of the South as the quaint, backward nation portrayed in the TV show* M*A*S*H.**

Add to this volatile mix the death of two South Korean schoolgirls, crushed to death under the wheels of a U.S. Army vehicle last June. By all accounts, this was a horrible accident—"a world-class tragedy," in the words of one American diplomat. Yet President Bush waited months before apologizing for the incident and then did so indirectly, through the American ambassador to Seoul. By contrast, when an American submarine collided with a Japanese fishing trawler off the coast of Hawaii in 2001, killing nine Japanese, Bush phoned Japan's prime minister to apologize and even led a moment of silence for the dead.

When a U.S. military tribunal found the servicemen not guilty of negligent homicide in South Korea, a firestorm of anti-American protests ensued, which helped Roh get elected. Yet today's anti-American movement is different from any such past movements in South Korea. It's much broader, attracting housewives and software engineers in addition to the scruffy college students who always have been reliable anti-American firebrands. And, in a sense, it's as much pro-Korean. South Koreans don't want to kill Americans. They don't even want the American troops to leave. A poll last month conducted by the South Korean branch of Gallup found that only 32 percent of South Koreans support a troop withdrawal. They just want some respect: Protesters constantly call for a more "mature and equal relationship" with Washington, a phrase they repeat like a mantra.

What does that mean? For starters, they say, revising the legal status of the 37,000 American troops based in South Korea. South Koreans complain that the American troops are above local law. That's true in Japan as well; the Status of Forces Agreements in both countries are virtually identical. But in Japan the American troops are practically invisible, unless you happen to live in Okinawa, an island in the far south of the Japanese archipelago where more than half of the American forces are based. In South Korea, the troops' sprawling base sits smack in the middle of Seoul, hoarding 630 acres of prime real estate in a massive and growing city and serving as a daily reminder to South Koreans that they are incapable of defending themselves. Many South Koreans say that making American troops punishable under South Korean law, and even possibly pulling some troops out of South Korea while maintaining America's military presence in other parts of the Pacific, would be a start. They also want Washington to treat Seoul as an equal partner in resolving problems with Pyongyang.

The United States is beginning to recognize that the forces for change in South Korea have acquired an unstoppable momentum. With little fanfare last month at the Pentagon, Defense Secretary Donald Rumsfeld and his South Korean counterpart Lee Jun agreed to review the entire U.S.–South Korean military alliance, a review that might result in a scaling back of America's troop presence in the South. America's pullout from the Philippines in the early '90s might serve as a model. At that time, anti-American sentiment ran high in the Philippines. Ten years later, facing an Islamic insurgency, the Philippines invited American troops back.

S. Korean President: Nothing to Worry About Relocation of U.S. Troops from Seoul[5]

BY SANG-HUN CHOE
THE ASSOCIATED PRESS, JANUARY 19, 2004

President Roh Moo-hyun has said the decision to pull all U.S. troops out of metropolitan Seoul will not weaken South Korea's security against North Korean military threats, as the city weighed a proposal to turn the base into a recreation space rivaling New York's Central Park.

"There is nothing to worry about it at all," Roh was quoted as saying by his office when he met leaders of the pro-government Uri Party Sunday evening.

"We have done our best" in our negotiations with the U.S. military, he said.

The agreement between the United States and South Korea to relocate 7,000 U.S. troops and family members from their base smack in the center of Seoul will make the South Korean capital free of foreign troops for the first time in a century.

Yet the move is a divisive issue.

To some, the base is a symbol of the U.S.–South Korean alliance that repelled a communist invasion during the 1950–53 Korean War and provided the security that made South Korea's economic growth possible.

South Korea's postwar generations, however, often see the foreign military presence in their capital as a slight to national pride. Others complain the 656-acre (262-hectare) base occupies prime real estate and worsens the city's chronic traffic congestion. Crimes involving U.S. soldiers further fuel anti-American sentiment.

What to do with the base after the U.S. military moves out is a matter of debate in Seoul. But a Metropolitan Government official said Monday the city is considering plans to turn the site into a commons area that would rival New York's 843-acre (337-hectare) Central Park.

Relocation costs are expected to total U.S.$3 billion to U.S.$4 billion and be covered by the South Korean government, a Foreign Ministry official said on condition of anonymity.

---

5. Reprinted with permission of The Associated Press.

Seoul's Yongsan, or "Dragon Hill," district has been occupied by foreign forces since 1882 when Chinese troops came to Seoul. Later Japanese troops took the area, as regional powers jockeyed for control over Korea.

U.S. forces came to Seoul in 1945 to disarm Japanese colonial troops at the end of World War II, later led U.N. forces during the Korean War and have remained as a deterrent against North Korea.

When the two allies announced Saturday they will pull the U.S. forces out of Seoul over the next three years, conservative South Koreans feared it would make South Korea more vulnerable to attacks from North Korea.

The South Korean government had asked that a contingent of as many as 1,000 troops remain. But that option foundered on a disagreement over how much land would be needed to support a contingent of that size.

Instead, 50 to 100 U.S. liaison personnel will stay, and the rest will move to an expanded U.S. facility about 45 miles (70 kilometers) south of Seoul.

Last June, the U.S. military also announced it would move its troops based near the Demilitarized Zone separating the two Koreas to bases south of Seoul.

The redeployments would put the U.S. troops out of the range of North Korean artillery and rockets, which can reach Seoul. It spurred fear in South Korea that the U.S. military would no longer serve as a "trip wire" in case of a North Korean invasion—taking immediate casualties and thus ensuring U.S. commitment to a fight.

Both U.S. and South Korean officials have tried to mitigate such fears, and note that the redeployment does not reduce the total number of 37,000 U.S. troops based in South Korea.

Pentagon strategists call the "trip wire" concept outdated, and say that the moves are aimed at strengthening U.S. defense capabilities on the peninsula and in the rest of the region.

The United States has announced a U.S.$11 billion package to improve U.S. military readiness on the peninsula. The plans include swift-action units, high-tech air surveillance and anti-missile systems, and high-speed transport that would carry quick contingents from U.S. troops based in Japan.

Tensions remain high on the Korean Peninsula over the communist North's nuclear weapons program. The United States, the two Koreas, Japan, China and Russia are trying to call a new round of six-nation talks aimed at dismantling the North's nuclear programs in return for possible economic aid and security guarantees.

S. Korea's Divisions[6]

By Michael Dorgan
San Jose Mercury News, January 11, 2003

Sipping a latte in Seoul's trendy downtown Myeong-dong district, 20-year-old Park Jin Woo pondered a paradox that has huge implications for South Korea, the United States and all of northeast Asia.

It's this: As South Korea's younger generation has grown more Western in recent years in its tastes and lifestyle, it has become increasingly anti-American.

The North Korean nuclear standoff has revealed deep strains within the once rock-solid U.S.–South Korean relationship. Underlying those strains is a generation gap in South Korea that pits a generally pro-American older generation against a younger generation increasingly suspicious of the United States and less worried by North Korea.

"Older people do not understand our clothing and our hairstyles," said Park, gesturing toward his own fashionably shaggy henna-dyed locks. "And older people, including my parents, do not believe that North Korea has changed its attitude. But younger people believe that North Korea will gradually—not suddenly, but gradually—change."

Seoul's Myeong-dong district, where Park was having coffee at Starbucks, is full of American fast-food restaurants and clothing franchises. Young Koreans on the streets would not look out of place in Chicago or San Francisco. Bookstores and record shops reflect a strong influence, if not dominance, of American culture.

But just a few blocks away at the fenced and fortified U.S. Embassy, which is perpetually surrounded by riot police to fend off protesters, young Koreans gather almost daily to denounce America.

Sometimes their numbers are small, sometimes large. One evening this week, only a few dozen showed up at a demonstration called to protest the acquittal of two U.S. soldiers involved in a road accident last summer that killed two teenage girls. On New Year's Eve, more than 10,000 gathered to demonstrate over the same issue. Many protesters at both events called for the withdrawal of all U.S. troops from South Korea.

The United States has no plans to withdraw its troops, because they are crucial to South Korea's security and the stability of northeast Asia, American officials say. But a U.S. official in Seoul, who asked that he not be identified, said Thursday that plans were

---

6. Article by Michael Dorgan from *San Jose Mercury News* January 11, 2003. Copyright © *San Jose Mercury News*. Reprinted with permission.

under way to move the command garrison out of the capital to lower the U.S. military's profile and ease tensions. The "future shape" of the U.S. role in South Korea's security is under study, the official added.

"The United States is a bigger threat to South Korea than North Korea is," said Han In Suk, a 17-year-old high school student who attended one of the protests despite orders from her parents not to go.

Han's anti-American sentiments are incomprehensible to Lee Sung Soo, a 76-year-old Korean War veteran who ran a small auto-parts business before he retired.

"I'm worried about the generation gap," he said. "The young guys are very simple in their thoughts. They don't know who keeps peace on the Korean Peninsula."

According to Lee, peace on the peninsula and prosperity in South Korea are in large part due to the security umbrella provided by the United States.

"If North Korea has nuclear weapons, it will destroy us," he said. "We need U.S. troops in Korea."

The generation gap between Han and Lee is explained partly by the vast difference in life experiences of older and younger South Koreans.

Those over 55 have painful memories of a brutal war in which more than 2 million people died, including 33,000 American soldiers. Those over 40 have vivid recollections of grueling poverty and hardship, as well as terrifying threats from North Korea.

South Koreans in their 20s and 30s have no experience of war. Most have not suffered privation.

Differences of opinion do not end there. Most older South Koreans still regard the United States as a protector that saved the country from an invasion by North Korea 53 years ago. They want the 37,000 U.S. military personnel who remain in South Korea to stay as a deterrent to North Korea.

A growing number of younger South Koreans, though, view the United States not as a protector but as a bully impeding unification of the Korean Peninsula.

"My parents suffered during the Korean War and they began to believe that South Korea has to depend on the United States," said Park, a computer-science major at Ajou University just outside of Seoul. "We were born after the South Korean economy began to develop, and we have begun to think that South Korea can survive on its own."

But the generation gap cannot be blamed entirely on different life experiences. It also is a byproduct of President Kim Dae Jung's "sunshine" policy, which for the past five years has promoted even-

> *The generation gap . . . is explained partly by the vast difference in life experiences of older and younger South Koreans.*

tual reunification of the divided Korean Peninsula through a process of aid, investment and dialogue with isolated and bankrupt North Korea.

The policy won President Kim a Nobel Peace Prize but has not produced many tangible results. However, it has led to a decline in the perception that the North is a threat, in large part because North Korea's propaganda machine has re-targeted most of its verbal attacks on Washington and Tokyo rather than Seoul.

The South Korean president, in his push for better relations with North Korea, has dangerously downplayed the military threat from North Korea, his critics say.

He has done so, they say, even though most of North Korea's million-member army remains offensively deployed near the South Korean border and even though North Korea's missiles have grown more numerous and lethal.

"The government is partly to blame for the generation gap," said Kyong Mann Jeon, an analyst at the Korea Institute for Defense Analysis, a government-funded research organization in Seoul.

He and others say Kim even downplayed the disclosure by the United States last fall that North Korea, by pursuing a secret uranium-enrichment program, had violated several international agreements not to develop nuclear weapons.

Jeon said the Kim administration apparently feared that a strong condemnation of North Korea would expose the failure of his approach toward the North and generate a voter backlash in last month's presidential election. Kim backed candidate Roh Moo Hyun, who campaigned on a "sunshine" policy platform.

Roh spoke to the anti-American sentiments held by young voters. He boasted of never having visited the United States and criticized politicians who had for "kowtowing" to the superpower.

It was a winning strategy. Roh, who will take office next month, won the election by winning support from the vast majority of voters in their 20s and 30s.

IV. Economy

Editor's Introduction

The differences between the economies of the two Koreas are staggering. The North Korean economy is on the brink of collapse. The country's leadership has focused its energies on policies of militarization since the Korean War, causing it to completely neglect the creation of policies geared towards strengthening or improving the economy. It is this disregard that has kept North Korea's economy and infrastructure stalled as the rest of the world has embraced the 21st century. On the other hand, South Korea's economy is the third largest in Asia. When South Korea recovered from the financial crisis of 1997–98, it never looked back and has continued to expand, especially through its foreign relations policies, which have benefited its economy. Chapter four examines the economic issues surrounding the Koreas. It broaches past events that have influenced the path each economy has taken, the role leadership has played, and each country's present economic situation. It also attempts to provide an outlook for what the future may hold for each economy should it proceed with its present initiatives.

"Korea's Economy Opens Up" by O. Yul Kwon begins the chapter, providing an introduction to South Korean economics and focusing on the time period surrounding the financial crisis of 1997–98. After discussing the events that led up to the difficulties and the specific reasons for South Korea's economic downfall, Kwon then turns his attention toward the reforms instituted by the South Korean government to prevent another economic collapse. The article continues with a look at the nation's recovery from the crisis and concludes with a prediction for its future economic standing.

While some Asian economies are still trying to regain their footing after the struggles of 1997–98, South Korea has made excellent progress in this area and is becoming a leader within the region. Stephen Schurr's "U.S. Investors Go Seoul-Searching in Spite of Strife" provides an overview of investment trends in South Korea, as well as the various opinions on investing in the South Korean market. Schurr discusses the benefits of investing in South Korea and why so many investors are attracted to that country's market, while also attempting to explain the reasons behind the prevailing skepticism held not only by some foreign investors, but also by the Korean people, who do not have much faith in their own market.

While South Korea focuses on economic development, North Korea's economy has remained stagnant and fixed since the war of 1950–53. It has yet to see any real forward movement in its economy, and because of its lack of initiatives, the country remains in dire straits. These dismal circumstances have forced the characteristically withdrawn nation to pull itself out of insolvency by looking outside its borders. "A Doomed Reform," from the *Harvard International Review*, reviews North Korea's entrance into the free market and its specific attempts to change its strategy, questioning whether these reforms are the best ones for the country or will prove even more disastrous down the road. Previous failures of the North to reform its economy are addressed, as well as the country's recent willingness to pursue diplomatic relations with other Asian countries during this time of economic hardship, in Mark Magnier's "N. Korea Is More Open, U.N. Says."

Korea's Economy Opens Up[1]

By O. Yul Kwon
Ivey Business Journal, September/October 2000

Foreign firms trying to enter the Korean market before the crisis of 1997 faced several obstacles. Extensive government intervention created policies that promoted and protected domestic industries. These policies also drew the chaebols, the intricately and closely linked industrial conglomerates, into powerful partnerships with the government. And a paternalistic employment system, embedded with complex social norms, helped entrench Korea's unique business structure and management system.

But though the structure was a strong one, it could not prevent the sudden economic crippling caused by the 1997 financial crisis. Fortunately, perhaps, the crippling was also a small blessing, unmistakably signalling that both the structure and the principles that supported the economy could not be sustained. The consequences for the Korean business community were huge, as dramatic policy shifts forced fundamental changes not only in how business was conducted but also in who conducted it. Today, the changes continue to have a considerable impact on foreign interests seeking to enter, or expand in, the Korean market.

The Business Environment: 1997

At the Korean government's request, the International Monetary Fund agreed to provide $58 billion in financial assistance to save Korea from defaulting on its foreign debt. The IMF imposed strict conditions and policies that are still forcing changes in Korea's business environment (all currency in U.S. dollars unless otherwise noted).

The causes of the 1997 financial crisis have been extensively researched and documented. They are primarily: (1) a loss of international competitiveness; (2) the chaebols' excessive expansion and diversification using debt capital; (3) an inefficient financial sector, with lax moral standards; (4) a lack of transparency in business and banking operations; and (5) an inflexible labour market. Each of these causes had its roots in the distinctive Korean business environment.

Korean companies' loss of international competitiveness was largely the result of the state's protection of domestic industries. Numerous government regulations distorted resource allocation and encouraged inefficient business operations. The government

---

1. One time permission to reproduce granted by Ivey Management Services on June 1, 2004.

pursued its export promotion and industrialization policy through a limited number of chaebols, by providing the latter with financial assistance and institutionalized privileges, and protecting them from international competitors and minority shareholders. Such policies generated an excessive concentration of economic power in the hands of a limited number of chaebols, and a collusive government-chaebol relationship. Because of their perceived infallibility, the chaebols relied mainly on debt capital from the domestic financial sector to expand and diversify This was a direct cause of the financial crisis.

However, the crisis was caused by more than the chaebols' excesses. For example, in order to control credit to execute its industrial policy, the government also controlled and protected financial institutions as both owner and regulator. Collusion between the government and the financial sector became common. At the same time, the financial sector's efficiency declined and the perception that bank failure was unlikely grew even stronger. This led to an undercapitalization in the financial sector. Under pressure from advanced countries, Korea liberalized the sector in the early 1990s. Almost immediately, banks borrowed excessively from the short-term, international capital markets and lent the money to chaebols for long-term projects. This policy was also a direct cause of the financial crisis. Collusion with the government and protection from any reform resulted in a lack of transparency in how the chaebols and banks were managed.

Finally, Korean labour was inflexible. This was more than just a cause of the financial crisis. It was also a strong feature of Korea's distinct business environment. Labour's failure to respond to changing domestic conditions helped raise labour costs rapidly and discouraged foreign investment. Both outcomes also helped reduce Korea's international competitiveness.

This brief analysis shows that the causes of the financial crisis were the very features that made Korea's business environment so distinctive and difficult for foreigners. Hence, the IMF's remedial measures required some fundamental shifts in what had become the defining features of Korea's business environment.

The Market Opens

The crisis forced the Korean government to begin dismantling its policy of protecting domestic industries, not only because the IMF required it to do so but also because of pressure from advanced countries, who wanted the Korean market to open up. Today, the government continues to liberalize trade regulations and harmonize import procedures with international standards. In fact, the government has made particular efforts to attract foreign direct investment [FDI]. It has switched the emphasis in its FDI policy to "promotion and assistance" from "restriction and control." Under the new Foreign Investment Promotion Act of November 1998, the government streamlined complicated administrative procedures by dismantling or relaxing more than 50 percent of the restrictions. It also introduced the so-called one-stop service system for inward FDI.

Mergers and acquisitions have been promoted in conjunction with liberalization. Before 1997, domestic or foreign investors were prohibited from acquiring Korean companies. However, takeover laws have been drastically

> *Before 1997, domestic or foreign investors were prohibited from acquiring Korean companies.*

liberalized since the crisis and hostile takeovers have been occurring freely. As a result of these measures to promote FDI and M&As, FDI in Korea reached a record high of $8.9 billion in 1998, compared to $3.2 billion in 1996. Of the total $8.9 billion FDI in 1998, M&A investment accounted for $4.7 billion, or 53.1 percent, indicating dramatic progress in establishing an investor-friendly business environment.

Since the crisis, Korea has also opened up a number of sectors to FDI; by the end of 1999, 99.4 percent of all industries were open to FDI. The business sectors liberalized since the 1997 crisis include financial services, securities markets, commodity exchanges, investment companies and trusts, real estate, golf course operation, grain processing, insurance-related businesses, petrol service stations, power generation and waterworks. Allowing foreigners to purchase land and other real estate for business and non-business purposes has also opened up the Korean distribution sector to foreigners. Discount retailers and chains such as Wal-Mart, Costco, Carrefour and the Price Club have already set up operations.

In accordance with the IMF's conditions, the financial sector has been restructured. This has increased the banking sector's independence from government, consolidated and strengthened the supervision of all financial institutions, liquidated a number of insolvent financial institutions and recapitalized viable ones. To increase transparency, the financial sector adopted international standards for disclosure and auditing. To improve management accountability, financial institutions established boards of directors whose members are selected by shareholders. In particular, restructuring has opened the financial sector for FDI and M&As and allowed competition from overseas financial institutions. Consequently, as of September 1999, substantial amounts of foreign capital were invested in Korean banks, and major foreign shareholders were participating in bank management. Indeed, in September 1999, a troubled bank (Korea First Bank) was sold to Newbridge Capital in the United States, marking a watershed in the Korean financial sector. The presence of foreign capital in the banking industry is likely to enhance its competitiveness, transparency, accountability and risk management practices. At the same time, it will stop the government from intervening in the financial sector.

Chaebol Reform

Reform of the chaebols has been pursued using the "five-plus three-point" principles that were agreed to by the chaebols and the government. The five principles refer to making management transparent, eradicating cross-debt payment guarantees among subsidiaries of the same chaebol, improving their financial structure, specializing in core businesses and improving corporate governance. The additional three points are intended to prevent the chaebols from dominating the non-bank financial sector, to prohibit cross-investment and illegal internal trading among subsidiaries, and to prevent abnormal wealth inheritance. Once completed, these agreements will enhance the chaebols' operating transparency, financial soundness, corporate governance, and ensure that they concentrate on their core competencies. They will also eliminate the institutionalized privileges that government had bestowed on the chaebols and address the endemic problem of collusion between the government and the chaebols. This will not only remedy the major causes of the financial crisis but also address the disadvantages foreign competitors experienced.

Some observers claimed that while the Korean economy was quite open, its society remained closed.

Substantial progress has already been made in reforming the chaebols along the five-plus three-point principles. At the same time, substantial foreign capital has flowed into Korean businesses. By the end of January 1999, the number of listed firms whose combined foreign interests exceeded the share of the largest domestic shareholder increased to 42. Foreign investors in Korean companies will require those companies to improve transparency, corporate governance and management efficiency This will in turn decrease government intervention and collusion. As government-chaebol collusion disappears, so will the systemic privileges bestowed on chaebols. As a result, chaebols' perception of infallibility will certainly fade away. One indication of this is the recent demise of the Daewoo group, the second-largest chaebol. In the absence of the privileges bestowed upon chaebols, financial institutions, which have in turn been penetrated by foreign capital, will lend to chaebols only if they have evidence of sound business operations. This will force chaebols to concentrate on their core competencies and to divest their marginal interests.

Opening Up a Closed Korea

In the past, some observers claimed that while the Korean economy was quite open, its society remained closed. Today, the minds of Korean people and society at large are becoming more open.

Through the bitter experience of the 1997 financial crisis and the ensuing economic setback, Koreans appear to have developed some appreciation of globalization and begun adapting to it. These same Koreans have come to realize that foreign investment is indispensable to economic recovery, and their attitudes toward foreign business and investment are changing. The fact that foreign retailers have been well received by the Korean public is one example that society is opening up. Once the business environment improves and operations become transparent and more competitive, business practices that rely on networks among Koreans will diminish.

Labour-Market Reform

The IMF policy package demands that labour be more flexible, and substantial progress has already been made. The labour laws that were amended in February 1998 have improved flexibility by allowing workforce retrenchment, part-time employment and flexible working hours. For the first time in Korean history, layoffs are allowed in the event of urgent management needs such as business transfers and M&As caused by extreme financial difficulty. A number of precedents demonstrating the social acceptance of layoffs have also been established, creating a new era for human resource management. Today, lifetime employment is no longer taken for granted. This amendment facilitates the restructuring that is necessary and allows firms to be more competitive. The employment adjustment system will also enhance the efficiency of labour management. Whereas in the past labour disputes arose largely over the issue of wage hikes, employment security is set to emerge as a major issue of contention in the future.

The configuration of the Korean labour market has changed remarkably since the revision of the labour laws. From 1996–1998, 65 percent of all domestic companies implemented workforce retrenchment. This has changed the proportion of full-time and part-time workers. The number of full-time workers decreased from 81.2 percent in 1996 to 57.7 percent by the end of 1998, while the number of part-timers increased from 18.8 percent to 42.3 percent during the same period. For the first time in history, the wage rate decreased in 1998. Due to downsizing and reduced wages, the personnel expenses of the 30 largest chaebols in 1998 decreased by 42 percent of what they were in 1997—a feat inconceivable before the crisis. As layoffs and workforce retrenchment become possible, militant union tactics will be mitigated.

Economic Policy: A Paradigm Shift

The industrial policy paradigm before the crisis can best be described as one of extensive state intervention, with consecutive five-year economic plans. Although intervention worked well until the late 1980s, it turned out to be the major underlying cause of the 1997 financial crisis. After the crisis forced policy-makers to realize the limitations of state intervention, the paradigm shifted. A government-led economy slowly began to be transformed into a market economy This shift has been reflected in the liberalization of domestic industries and the ongoing institutional and structural reform of financial institutions, the chaebols and the labour market. At the same time, the public sector has been reformed to enhance its efficiency. The government has already abolished about 50 percent of the regulations that served as tools of state intervention. Also, the central government plans to reduce the number of its employees by 11.9 percent by the end of 2000; local governments will cut their employee numbers by 20.2 percent by 2002.

Changes in the Korean Management System

Developments in Korea's business environment after the 1997 financial crisis have substantially changed management practices. Ongoing reform of businesses and banks and the elimination of chaebols' privileges and their collusion with government have meant that Korean companies and banks can no longer act as monopolies. They have to compete against foreign counterparts who are well equipped with capital and technology. The myth that big companies and banks would never fail has already disappeared. In order to survive, therefore, Korean companies will need to operate as efficiently as their foreign competitors. Under these circumstances, Korean companies will not be able to retain their traditional management system, although that part of the system that is deeply ingrained in Korean culture is unlikely to disappear easily.

For the sake of survival, Korean companies will need to replace clan management with management by efficient professionals. Labour's flexibility will eliminate the costly and inefficient convention of guaranteeing lifetime employment. The seniority system with a long hierarchical structure will not survive in the long term under increasing international competition. As job security at domestic companies declines and lifetime employment disappears, unions' militant tactics will be mitigated. Furthermore, the loyalty of employees towards companies will abate, undermining the practice of top-down decision making and autocratic leadership.

Foreign firms will find it easier to operate in Korea not only because of the change in the Korean management system, but also because of the increasing availability of competent workers who will accept employment. As the myth of chaebols' infallibility disappears and job security in domestic companies declines, Korean workers' preference for working for domestic firms rather than foreign ones will decline. Once laying off workers becomes a common practice among Korean companies, early-retired middle managers will be readily available for foreign companies. Talented female workers will remain an important source of recruitment for foreign companies.

As foreign companies and investors come to play an increasingly important role in the Korean economy, the importance of personal relationships in business operations will diminish, and the existing business networks will change as a result. Under the scrutiny of foreigners, personal relationships may not influence business operations, as they did so powerfully in the past. For the sake of their survival, many Korean suppliers and financial institutions will volunteer to be incorporated into the industrial network formed by foreign companies.

Economic Prospects
The Korean economy has been recovering since 1999, and for a number of reasons. These include an extension on short-term maturities on short-term foreign debt; restored macroeconomic stability; export expansion due to the depreciated currency value; a more accommodating monetary and fiscal policy; a broad range of structural reforms to establish a more market-oriented economy; the restoration of foreign confidence in the Korean economy, and increases in foreign capital inflows. Added to these is the econ-

---

As the Korean economy advances further, it will become increasingly difficult for Korea to attract foreign technology.

---

omy's resilience, evident in its recovery from a number of setbacks in the past. The 1997 financial crisis has proven to be a force that has united Koreans in the cause of helping the economy recover and prosper. Above all, the economic fundamentals, including the high savings rate, a well-educated workforce and advanced production infrastructure, remain sound. This series of developments contributed to rapid economic recovery in 1999.

The Korean economy is unlikely to grow in the medium term as quickly as it did in the past, at seven to nine percent a year. The potential growth rate will decline due to the slower growth of factor inputs. As the economy matures, national savings and investment rates will moderate, and in view of recent developments in demography and education, the human capital accumulation rate will also slow. Finally, as the Korean economy advances further, it will become increasingly difficult for Korea to attract foreign technology.

As the economy matures in the medium term, not only will the growth rate slow, but its industrial structure will change. Until 1997, Korea supported the manufacturing sector with massive investment and protected it from international competition, while it neglected the service sector. As the economy is liberalized further, the service sector will develop and expand at a relatively faster pace. In particular, Korea has realized how fragile existing industries are and how important it is to develop high technology and knowledge-intensive industries. Hence, the government has already highlighted the need to strengthen the knowledge base as a critical part of its national development strategy. As Korea is far behind advanced countries in high technology and knowledge-intensive industries, it is eagerly seeking foreign partners to develop them.

The Korean economy certainly is recovering from the crisis and for different reasons. One is the success of the institutional and structural reforms, which has in turn raised the confidence of foreign investors in the Korean economy. There is also the prospect that the economy will continue to grow at a moderate rate in the medium term, alongside renewed optimism that the Korean economy is now transforming itself into a knowledge-based economy The implications of doing business in Korea, for both domestic and foreign firms, are clear. The Korean market is now wide open and it is markedly easier to do business there than ever before. But it is also more competitive than ever. There is thus a major business opportunity for companies with proprietary technology and insights into the Korean system to participate productively in the new direction of the Korean economy.

U.S. Investors Go Seoul-Searching in Spite of Strife[2]

By Stephen Schurr
Financial Times, March 22, 2004

A maxim from global investor Sir John Templeton recommends investors buy into a market when "there's blood in the streets." In the case of South Korea, fisticuffs in parliament may suffice.

Earlier this month, a melee broke out on the floor of South Korea's National Assembly after a vote to impeach reform-minded President Roh Moo-Hyun. U.S. investors with their eyes on Seoul added political instability to a list of uncertainties—the fate of North Korea, concerns about corporate governance and reform and the high levels of consumers with credit card–fuelled debt woes.

Despite these concerns, money managers remain confident the political situation will be resolved and that Korea is one of the world's best bargain-hunting opportunities. "The Korean market remains attractive at these levels," says Paul Matthews, founder of the Matthews Asian Funds family and manager of the Matthews Korea fund. While Mr. Matthews and others do not think politics in Seoul will resolve themselves overnight, "the market isn't very demanding in its multiples."

The Seoul market has been one of the great success stories of the past few years. The Korea Composite Index (Kospi) has surged more than 60 percent over the past year and returned 8.5 percent a year on average over the past five years. On a valuation basis, the Kospi still looks very cheap. Its forward price-to-earnings multiple is currently 11.8, little more than half as expensive as the U.S. stock market.

Some sceptics say the low valuations are not tempting enough. "While there is genuine earnings growth in Korea, the low valuations are justified," says Edmund Harriss of the Guinness Atkinson Asia Focus fund. Mr. Harriss says concerns about the banking sector and consumer weakness have led him to cut back on his exposure to South Korea.

Of course, a developing market such as South Korea may not merit the richer valuations of a firmly established economy such as the U.S., even though political impeachment and corporate governance scandals do have a familiar ring to U.S. investors. Meanwhile, longtime Korea watchers note there has been genuine

---

reform in the Korean markets, not as much as investors might hope for in banking and among the chaebols that dominate Korean industry, but reform nonetheless.

Mr. Matthews notes that many Korean groups such as Korea Telecom are considering increasing dividend payouts, which would further entice U.S. investors. "There are plenty of reasons why stocks are cheap," says Jamie Doyle, portfolio manager for the Causeway International Value fund.

"But as we look across the globe, we keep coming back to Korea as a source for some really cheap stocks—and these are stocks that are world beaters."

The biggest of the "world beaters" is Samsung Electronics, which makes up 22 percent of the Kospi. With a P/E in the high single digits, it may be the world's cheapest tech stock; other semiconductor companies trade at multiples of 25 to 35 times earnings and have worse growth prospects.

"Samsung has consistently generated 20 to 30 percent return on equity, which is extraordinarily tough to do in 'commodity tech' markets," Mr. Doyle says.

"We keep coming back to Korea as a source for some really cheap stocks."—Jamie Doyle, portfolio manager

---

Indeed, efficiency, innovation and cost-containment policies helped Samsung reap profits in its D-Ram chips business when rivals such as Micron and Infineon were awash in red ink. Meanwhile, the company's leading role in high-growth areas, from liquid crystal display technology to flash memory, put it in good stead for the next several years.

For money managers, Samsung has become the Seoul equivalent of Cisco in the 1990s, when the saying went, "nobody gets fired for owning Cisco." Even Korea bears such as Mr. Harriss own Samsung (he also favours steel giant Posco).

Another trend working in Samsung's favour is the gush of foreign money flowing into Korea. In the near term, large-cap companies—especially Samsung—tend to draw the largest portions of new cash.

There are dichotomies within the Korean market, several of which pivot around issues of foreign and domestic demand.

First, the nation has relied fairly heavily on exporting business, with manufacturing sectors performing well while the domestic economy remains fragile. The banking system is in need of reform, and the recent credit-happy consumer binge has left 3 million Koreans in default on their debts.

Investors cautious about Korea's prospects think this trend will continue, while Mr. Matthews believes it will shift as the domestic economy strengthens.

The other dichotomy has to do with investor perceptions at home and abroad. Foreign investors have bought into the Korean growth story. The market is nearly 50 percent owned by foreigners, who withdrew little money amid the political flare-up this month.

However, individual Korean investors have little confidence in their own market, due in part to cynicism about the chaebols, the perception of crony capitalism and painful memories of the crisis that crushed Seoul's markets in 1997.

With the exception of active short-term traders, Koreans have abandoned the stock market almost entirely in favour of bonds that return 3 to 4 percent. If reform takes hold and Korea's growing middle class decides to put more money into stocks, it could be good news for the Kospi.

Oddly, the biggest bugbear about Seoul for many U.S. investors is one that domestic investors do not worry about nearly as much: South Korea's neighbour to the north. U.S. investors see tensions between their government and North Korea over nuclear weapons as a potential destabilising force for Seoul and its markets. But Mr. Matthews says Korean investors are much less concerned about sabre-rattling by the North.

As for internal politics, while the impeachment process—and the brawl that the U.S. media broadcast for days—will be a cloud that lingers over Korea for the short term, positive developments may emerge from the affair. The growing opinion is that the conservatives overreached with the impeachment, now in the hands of the Constitutional Court, which has 180 days to reach its decision.

Han Sung Joo, South Korea's ambassador to the U.S., told an audience at the Asia Society in New York that protests against the impeachment of a reform-minded president may mean the party that opposed the vote would notch strong gains in the April 15 parliamentary elections. If so, the impeachment drive will lose even more steam and the push to reform fully Seoul's markets may be the victor.

Wishful thinking? Perhaps. If so, U.S. investors still have a P/E of 11.8 to fall back on.

A Doomed Reform[3]

By Harpal Sandhu
Harvard International Review, Spring 2003

After the fall of the Soviet Union, world politics shifted away from the conflict between communism and capitalism that had characterized much of the 20th century. But in northeast Asia lies one of the last relics of the Cold War and the last Stalinist state, the Democratic People's Republic of Korea, commonly referred to as North Korea. Ruled by a dictatorship that sheltered its citizens from the putative poison of decadent Western culture and influence, North Korea existed in almost complete isolation from the West for decades. However, recent economic reforms and attempts at fostering political discourse with its neighbors mark a conspicuous departure from previous foreign and domestic policy for this international enigma. Once a staunch proponent of communism and national self-reliance, or *juche*, North Korea has devalued its currency 70-fold, allowed prices and wages to be determined by markets, partially eliminated rationing, and announced the creation of a Chinese-style special economic zone (SEZ) open to foreign investment. This arrangement is radically different from traditional North Korean socialism.

On the political front, North Korea has re-opened dialogue with Japan, admitted abducting 13 Japanese citizens in the 1970s and 1980s, begun limited de-mining of the Demilitarized Zone (DMZ), and agreed to the creation of the first railroad link between the two Koreas since World War II. As promising as these developments appear, however, North Korea is unlikely to begin an immediate economic revival like the one China experienced two decades ago. North Korea's unusual new economic reforms and diplomatic initiatives are misguided attempts to reinvigorate a decaying economy and curry international favor and concessions. In the long run, many of its economic changes and diplomatic maneuvers may prove self-defeating.

Only a serious crisis within the economy could persuade North Korea's government to change its socialist ways. The dramatic decline of the North Korean economy began with the loss of Soviet subsidies and trade following the collapse of the Soviet Union in 1991. North Korea's exports plummeted while its leader, President Kim Il-Sung, refused to reduce imports. Furthermore, military expenditures continued at a level that enabled this country of slightly more than 22 million people to maintain the third largest

---

3. Reprinted by permission of the Harvard International Review. From "A Doomed Reform: North Korea Flirts with the Market" by Harpal Sandhu, Spring 2003.

army in the world. The results were disastrous—gross domestic product (GDP) fell by 50 percent between 1992 and 1997. Worst of all, a devastating famine engulfed North Korea, forcing the reclusive government to appeal to the World Food Programme for aid. While help did come, the humanitarian group Doctors Without Borders estimates that at least 10 percent of the population perished. With a decimated population, a decade of economic recession, and a dearth of communist allies, North Korea has begun to infuse capitalist elements into its supposed workers' paradise.

Getting Ahead

Logic would dictate that North Korea, which is devoid of any substantial capitalist experience in the last half-century, should begin reform with baby steps. Instead, the government has embarked on several dramatic reforms. Beginning in summer 2002, the North Korean government lifted most price controls and allowed market forces to set prices by supply and demand. Although initial results do not necessarily predict the future, the new policies created huge discrepancies and asymmetries in the economy. While average wages increased 200 times, the price of rice rose 400 times, diesel fuel 40 times, and electricity 60 times. Furthermore, the North Korean government has made no move to integrate private enterprise into the economy, an omission that could cause catastrophic problems in the future. Allowing demand to run rampant while limiting supply by suppressing private enterprise only exacerbates inflation. On the other hand, in a move that foreshadowed the new SEZ and desire for foreign investment, the government slashed the official value of the North Korean currency from the rate of 2.15 won to the U.S. dollar to 150 won to the U.S. dollar. The devaluation of the won to better reflect its market value has been hailed as a wise decision that should help increase trade.

North Korea has begun to infuse capitalist elements into its supposed workers' paradise.

North Korea's effort at reform is reminiscent of *perestroika*, the late 1980s restructuring that Premier Mikhail Gorbachev implemented in the Soviet Union shortly before its collapse in 1991. With decentralization occurring in a large number of industries, managers were suddenly presented with decisions that they lacked the experience to make. Similarly, the rapid pace of change in North Korea has forced the general public to confront many unfamiliar decisions on a daily basis. Workers without any experience in budgeting will no longer be provided with all their food and shelter by a state rationing system. As demonstrated by the fate of the Soviet Union, these transition problems can prove stubbornly persistent.

North Korean reform has also taken on a decidedly Chinese twist. In September 2002, North Korea announced plans to develop a version of China's SEZs in order to attract foreign investment.

This new zone is to be located in Sinuiju, which lies along the Yalu River bordering China on the west coast of the Korean peninsula. The plan calls for 500,000 current Sinuiju residents to be replaced by 200,000 technically skilled new residents from North Korea and China. Estimates place the shipping capacity of the 50-square-mile region at 12 million tons per year, and the nearby Supung hydro-electric power plant will accommodate all of the region's energy needs. The North Korean government has declared that Sinuiju would be a semi-autonomous region with its own legislature and the right to private property. Although the government eventually retracted a promise to allow foreigners to enter the region without visas, there will be other incentives to lure foreign investment. The U.S. dollar will be an official currency and the income tax will be capped at 14 percent. This economic gambit is frequently compared to China's first special economic zone in Shenzhen in 1979. A sleepy fishing village prior to the reforms, Shenzhen ballooned to a population of seven million. Its success convinced China to launch five more zones of the same type. Just over a decade into this capitalist experiment, the five zones in existence in 1991 were responsible for 15 percent of China's U.S.$57 billion in trade that year.

Of course, North Korea seeks to duplicate this kind of success. But there are important distinctions to be made between the situations of Shenzhen and Sinuiju. The first distinction is geographical. Shenzhen, as well the four other zones, is located in the south of China in close proximity to Hong Kong. Already a bustling and successful metropolis, Hong Kong became Shenzhen's primary trading partner. Sinuiju, on the other hand, has no immediate neighbors, aside from South Korea, with the wealth to invest heavily in the region. However, South Koreans are skeptical of investment because of horror stories about bureaucratic inertia in the North as well as weariness of risky investments since the 1997 Asian financial crisis.

Underlying most Western investment in Shenzhen was the hope of using the SEZ as a gateway to the gigantic consumer market in China. No such motive exists in the case of Sinuiju. Instead of one billion potential Coca-Cola drinkers in North Korea, there are closer to 22 million. This number is probably not large enough to persuade Western businesses to invest in Sinuiju, especially considering the country's atrocious record of entrepreneurial ventures.

Former Failures

The 1990s featured two spectacular failures of private enterprise and entrepreneurship in North Korea. In fact, the Sinuiju project would not be the first time that the North Korean government has established a special economic zone. In 1996, it created the Rajin-Sonbong Economic and Trade Zone (RSETZ) on the northeastern tip of the peninsula. Surrounded by barbed wire in order to shut out North Korean citizens, the RSETZ occupied a seemingly promising location. The disconnected Sino-Mongolian railroad, if completed, would have made the RSETZ the terminus of a trans-Eurasian railroad. Moreover, the cost of labor in the RSETZ was appreciably lower than in the Chinese coastal cities. Also, it was perennially free of ice and very close to Japan. All that was lacking was additional infrastructure, a problem that was overcome at Shenzhen. To this day, however, Rajin-Sonbong remains a desolate place. The fact that nothing became of the RSETZ suggests that there are inherent problems with North Korea's ability to attract investment. The potential benefits to international investors of expanding to the general North Korean public do not outweigh the risks of investing in an unpredictable international pariah.

While the RSETZ was a solely North Korean venture, there also have been joint attempts to open North Korea to the world. In 1998, the Hyundai Corporation of South Korea cooperated with Pyongyang on an ambitious plan to make North Korea's scenic Mount Kumgang a tourist attraction. Located on the eastern Korean coast just north of the DMZ, Mount Kumgang was originally viewed as a beacon of hope in the otherwise dark prospects of reunification.

Benefits . . . of expanding to the general North Korean public do not outweigh the risks of investing in an unpredictable international pariah.

Unfortunately, the project has been a commercial calamity. The six missile launchers, searchlights, and armed guards littering the mountain hardly make the resort an ideal place to relax. Hyundai reduced the number of ferries to the resort from four per week to one per week, and even that single boat is not filled to capacity. The resort is in such dire straits that Hyundai's hopes of profit have vanished, and the South Korean government must subsidize it in order to keep alive this meager step toward reunification.

Strained Relations

Pyongyang has also emerged from its typical isolationism to engage diplomatically with its neighbors. This newfound openness in diplomacy comes, perhaps not coincidentally, at a time of crippling economic hardship and consequent reform. Indeed, the North Korean government seems to believe that admitting past transgressions gives them some leverage to force concessions to aid its ailing economy. The 1994 nuclear crisis reinforced this pattern of behavior. Pyongyang openly declared that it was in violation of the 1968 Treaty on the Non-Proliferation of Nuclear Weapons and agreed to weapons inspections that have never taken place. In return, they were promised shipments of fuel oil and U.S. assistance in the construction of two light-water nuclear reactors. Thus, when North Korean officials admitted in fall 2002 to a revived nuclear program, they may have been simply repeating previous tactics. However, the adverse Western reaction to that revelation indicates the strong possibility of a diplomatic miscalculation on the part of President Kim Jong-Il.

A similar line of thought can be applied to Pyongyang's surprising approach to Japan. Meeting with Japanese Prime Minister Junichiro Koizumi in September 2002, Kim conceded that a government agency had abducted 13 Japanese citizens during the 1970s and 1980s and subsequently refused to return the children of some of the Japanese nationals. Naturally, the Japanese government was outraged by the news and has ruled out any economic aid so long as the children remain in North Korea.

One can easily understand the deterioration of relations between North Korea and its rivals. However, relations with its ally China have also been tried recently. First and foremost, Pyongyang never consulted China about the special economic zone in Sinuiju, which lies on the Sino-Korean border. Apparently, the Chinese government is concerned that residents of Dandong, China, which is connected by bridge to Sinuiju, will flock to the new capitalist enclave in order to gamble. Furthermore, a statement by China's Foreign Ministry was coldly diplomatic in commenting on the Sinuiju experiment. "We have followed a path of socialism with Chinese characteristics," the Ministry reported. "Such a road is not necessarily suited to other countries' conditions."

But the most cogent evidence that China disapproves of Sinuiju lies in its arrest of Yang Bin, the man hired to govern Sinuiju, just one week after the government announced his appointment. Yang, whose net worth was estimated at U.S.$900 million by *Forbes* magazine, made his fortune in horticulture and took advantage of relaxed immigration laws in the wake of the 1989 student demonstrations of Tiananmen Square in order to gain Dutch citizenship. Although he has confessed to owing U.S.$1.2 million in back taxes to a Chinese provincial government, the timing of his arrest warrants interest. Beijing could have brought the evidence of Yang's criminal activities to Pyongyang's attention before taking action. Instead, his arrest took place just as North Korea was basking in the limelight of attention from the international media. Clearly, there is friction between North Korea and one of its few remaining allies.

The divergence in results between Soviet *perestroika* and the Chinese reforms is staggering. One state no longer exists, while the other continues to flourish. North Korea's reforms more closely resemble Gorbachev's rash and rapid *perestroika* than the incremental and reserved approach of Chinese leader Deng Xiaoping. Though such a comparison is not encouraging for the future of North Korea's current government, at least Pyongyang has taken the chance of loosening its grip on power in order to try to rejuvenate its crumbling economy. However, North Korea runs the risk of overturning whatever gains it may make from these economic changes. If its odd and mysterious diplomatic initiatives backfire, the state could be deprived of the international backing it so desperately seeks.

N. Korea Is More Open, U.N. Says[4]

BY MARK MAGNIER
LOS ANGELES TIMES, NOVEMBER 21, 2003

International aid groups operating in North Korea said Thursday that the isolated communist country had become slightly more open in recent months as economic reforms show modest signs of taking hold.

Humanitarian workers at a news conference here said the shift appeared to go beyond officials in Pyongyang and included school principals, hospital administrators and government workers, even in remote provinces.

"It manifests itself in many small ways," said Richard Corsino, U.N. World Food Program director for North Korea. "You see it in the sort of questions you're able to ask and the information you get on hunger and employment."

An easing signal probably came from on high, aid workers said. North Korea maintains a cult around its leader, Kim Jong Il, who took over after his father died nearly a decade ago.

"In a country like [North Korea], people don't suddenly wake up one day and decide to be more open," Corsino said.

Representatives from five United Nations agencies appealed for $221 million in international aid to fund relief programs next year. About $192 million of that would go to the WFP to feed 6.5 million people, they said.

The good news, they said, is that North Korea's economy has stabilized and its harvest is up for the third year in a row. There's a local market in Pyongyang, more small enterprises, and more consistent power and water supplies, at least in big cities. There's even a cellphone network. The government's push to plant two cereal crops a year is yielding more food. And the number of malnourished children has dropped.

The bad news is that North Korea still faces major food shortages and extensive distribution problems, with adverse consequences for children and pregnant women. "One-third of mothers are still malnourished," said Pierrette Vu Thi, UNICEF's Pyongyang representative, and "70,000 children are still at immediate risk of death without hospital care."

Though Pyongyang's modest steps to ease wage and price controls have helped the economy, they have also made food more expensive. Donor countries, meanwhile, are less interested in giving aid because of political concerns and because of competing needs in Afghanistan, southern Africa and Iraq.

According to U.N. figures, the U.S. remains the largest aid donor to North Korea, contributing $31.1 million so far this year.

Aid workers said it's hard to tell from inside North Korea that the country is in a global standoff over its self-declared nuclear weapons program. A second round of negotiations on the issue is tentatively set for mid-December in Beijing.

The humanitarian groups said that their view of changes in the country was by definition anecdotal and that they did not have any particular insight into the government's thinking. But they're now able to travel to 163 of North Korea's 206 counties, they said, which contain 86 percent of the population. And even though trips must be approved in advance, workers said, they have wide latitude to travel within a province once they get there.

The number of trips rejected by the authorities has dropped sharply, they said, and the government is far more forthcoming with employment, health and malnutrition data.

"There are less barriers, and there's much more willingness to share information than before," said Eigil Sorensen, the World Health Organization's representative in Pyongyang.

Reports persist that U.N. food aid is diverted to the military. Corsino said there was little doubt that Pyongyang's first priority was to feed its soldiers.

But it does so with food aid from South Korea and China, he maintained, which place no restrictions on where the food goes, leaving the international community confident that its supplies were not being diverted.

V. Military Strategies

Editor's Introduction

Though progress is being made to promote peace on the Korean peninsula, tensions still run high. The war-like atmosphere that exists at the DMZ is a driving factor for militarization on both sides, but especially the North. When the Cold War ended, North Korea lost one of its closest allies—the Soviet Union. Having only itself to rely upon for protection in this newly altered world, North Korea sought out a policy of intense militarization to level the playing field with South Korea, which is bolstered by the presence of U.S. troops on its side of the 38th parallel. South Korea, on the other hand, has until recently welcomed U.S. troops, which guarantee protection from the communist North, should the need arise. North Korea's recent admission of nuclear capabilities has further unsettled South Korea and the United States, who now worry about a potential nuclear conflict despite North Korea's declaration that its arms buildup is only a deterrent against U.S. aggression. Talks began in 2003 to convince North Korea to eliminate its nuclear stockpile, but with no agreement having yet been reached, both North and South remain prepared for war. Chapter five examines the two Koreas' military strategies, including North Korea's nuclear agenda, the effect of its arms buildup on the region, and the arms reduction talks, as well as future concerns accompanying this volatile situation.

"A Fragile Peace" by Peter Worthington begins the chapter with a discussion of South Korea's armed forces. Worthington examines the role of the U.S. in South Korea, especially concerns over American troop placement, and he looks at specific incidents within the South Korean military that reveal a lack of discipline among that country's troops. Despite the recent scandals that have surfaced surrounding South Korea's military, the South still has an edge over the North in terms of conventional weapons. More technologically advanced, with healthier, better educated soldiers, South Korea seems to have several key advantages, many of which are discussed in "South Korean Military Capability Reportedly Far Superior to North's," from the *BBC Summary of World Broadcasts*. The article reviews the exceedingly sophisticated nature of the South Korean defense forces in comparison to their Northern counterparts, while a sidebar compares statistics on each country's forces.

To compensate for its military deficiencies, North Korea has sought a policy of militarization to which it has recently added nuclear capability. The final half of this chapter discusses North Korea's announcement that it has weapons of mass destruction, how confirmation of the program's existence has already affected the east Asian sphere of influence, and the impact it could have in the future. CNN's Lou Dobbs reviews the kinds of nuclear weapons

North Korea now possesses and the international pressure on the North to disarm in his article for *U.S. News & World Report* "Nuclear Nightmare." Then, Thomas Omestad et al., in "A Balance of Terror," examine the concerns of world leaders that an arms race could develop throughout Asia should countries such as Taiwan and Japan feel threatened by North Korea's nuclear potential. The final article in this chapter, "Talks on North Korea Nuclear Program End" from *The Associated Press*, covers the negotiations with the Kim regime aimed at the dismantling of North Korea's nuclear program, and examines the next steps planned now that these sets of talks have ended. A timeline offers an overview of tensions that have arisen since North Korea's withdrawal from the Nuclear Nonproliferation Treaty in 1993.

A Fragile Peace[1]

By Peter Worthington
The Toronto Sun, August 25, 2003

The big debate going on in South Korea at the moment, is not whether North Korea will stage a sneak attack or use whatever nuclear weapons it may have, but whether the U.S. Army is doing the right thing by planning to remain in the South instead of staying poised along the 38th parallel.

Not many seriously think an attack by the North is imminent. They see threats by Kim Jong Il as a ploy to get more aid from the West, and from South Korea, where the desire for reunification blocks out logic.

"We are brothers and we want to re-unite," cry young protesters who ignore history.

That said, there is no serious dispute about North Korea being an "Axis of Evil" as defined by President George W. Bush. It's a ghastly regime in control, and everyone knows it.

Fear of American troops being withdrawn from the front and from Seoul, is motivated partly by almost constant demonstrations that ebb and flow outside the U.S. base of Yongsan. Being resented, even by a loony minority, is uncomfortable for Americans.

The rationale is that if U.S. forces are back from the demilitarized zone (DMZ), out of the range of artillery (but not missiles) that can target Seoul, the Americans can counter-attack with great force if the North dares attack.

Morale in Doubt

This sounds logical, but is it realistic? Koreans want, if they're subjected to a surprise attack, to have the Americans suffer casualties too—a sort of "tripwire" to guarantee a response to provocations.

Critics point to the changing world since the North attacked 53 years ago in 1950. South Korea is no longer defenseless. It has a considerable army of nearly half a million, superbly armed and technologically light-years more advanced than North Korea's million-man army.

---

1. Article by Peter Worthington from *The Toronto Sun* August 25, 2003. Copyright © *The Toronto Sun*. Reprinted with permission.

At question is how disciplined and determined the South Korean military is. Such questions don't arise with the North's military, which gives the impression of fanatic zeal. The morale of South Korea's army is in doubt.

> *As more "democracy" has taken root in Korea, so discipline has grown lax.*

All that outsiders usually see of the South Korean army are those handpicked, tall, physically intimidating South Korean soldiers, all experts in taekwondo, standing legs apart, fists clenched, staring menacingly at their small, robot-like counterparts in North Korea at Panmunjon.

At ceremonies, South Korean soldiers look scrubbed and smart in well-pressed, clean uniforms.

A deeper look is more disquieting.

The *Korea Times* recently had a disturbing editorial: "Military Discipline in Jeopardy." The editorial wondered, "How can people sleep amid national security worries?"

It outlined problems that outsiders know little about, like a rise in sex crimes. It cited the case of a private committing suicide after being sexually assaulted by a corporal. An army doctor was the centre of a scandal after kissing a nurse who didn't want to be kissed.

A Korean colonel was arrested this summer and charged with sexually harassing a 21-year-old private some 10 times. When a female Korean captain beat the bejesus out of an enlisted man who broke into her tent and sexually assaulted her, she was charged as well as the private. She apparently used unnecessary force to defend herself!

A general is up on a charge for accepting bribes from a construction company.

Such incidents previously never made the media. As more "democracy" has taken root in Korea, so discipline has grown lax.

An evaluation system has been introduced into the Korean army, whereby junior ranks assess the performance of their superiors—which has led to superiors easing up on discipline and standards to curry favour for a positive rating from those they command.

It's not hard to see pitfalls in this policy.

"Why introduce this formula in the military?" the *Korea Times* rhetorically asks. "It is essential for soldiers to be obedient to their superiors."

The newspaper urges that the military high command be held accountable for the "never-ending crimes and degradation of discipline."

The newspaper says, correctly, that problems in the army should be a "national issue," and not regarded as a "simple military one."

South Korea has conscription—every youth must serve two years, during which time he is paid about $22 a month—enough for cigarettes. Pay for the regular army is comparable to what could be earned in civilian life.

Conscription is becoming less and less popular among the young, many of whom now feel it's an impediment in their lives, and an obstacle to the cause of reunification with the "brothers" from the North—which it probably is.

Meanwhile, Kim Jong Il amends his agenda as necessary, and apparently has agreed to multilateral talks with neighbouring countries, and not just the U.S. as he once insisted. Japan, South Korea, Russia and China will now be involved—a small diplomatic triumph for the U.S.

No Gratitude Shown

As for humanitarian aid to the North, ironic as it seems, the U.S., which views North Korea as part of the "Axis of Evil," has been the largest single donor of aid—nearly $63.5 million (37.7 percent of the total $188.1 million given by the international community).

As well, the U.S. has given North Korea another $63 million in humanitarian aid through various U.N. agencies—55 percent of that total.

South Korea gives more than $65 million in humanitarian aid to its former "enemy" (which consistently snipes at its benefactor). Canada is donating $2.6 million this year, compared to $3.1 million last year through the Canadian International Development Agency.

Despite North Korea's dependency on foreign aid—which is suspected of going mostly to the dinner plates of the military and elite instead of to starving people—it shows neither gratitude nor appreciation, either in words or deeds. Instead, it issues threats for more.

The North Korean newspaper *Rodong Sinmun* and the magazine *Kulloja*, organs of the Central Committee, have warned that "the imperialists . . . through ideological and cultural infiltration" seek to destroy socialist states, just "as they undermined the Soviet Union."

To North Korean communists: "The imperialist's ideological and cultural poisoning is a means of aggression and intervention shrouded in the cloak of 'cooperation' and 'interchange.'"

If that's how they regard foreign aid and peaceful overtures, it makes one wonder why we keep pandering to Kim Jong Il, who seeks victory, not peaceful co-existence.

South Korean Military Capability Reportedly Far Superior to North's[2]

BBC Summary of World Broadcasts, October 8, 1999

The fighting ability of the DPRK [Democratic People's Republic of Korea] was recently found to lag absolutely behind that of the ROK [Republic of Korea] due to its serious economic difficulties and superannuated weapons systems.

According to a collection of troop educational materials published recently by the Office of Troop Information and Publication Affairs, Ministry of National Defence, the ROK stands far superior to the DPRK in actual military strength, as the DPRK military generally lags behind the ROK military in terms of the shape of its servicemen, combat ability, equipment performance, national strength, and joint defence preparedness.

This contradicts what was disclosed in a mid-term national defence plan announced by the defence ministry last March, which said in part that ROK war ability stands at a mere 79 percent of the DPRK's level, and that the ratio is set to be raised to 88 percent by 2004 by investing 26.7331 trillion won in force improvement programmes over the next five years.

Comparison of the battle ability of North and South Korea as disclosed by the Office of Troop Information and Publication Affairs shows that ROK troops measure 171 cm in height and 66 kg in weight on the average, whereas the average height and weight of DPRK troops are 162 cm and 48 kg. This indicates that DPRK troops can hardly be a match to ROK troops in close or drawn-out battles in emergency.

At the same time, DPRK troops are not properly educated and trained due to the shortage of such military supplies as petroleum and ammunition as well as to frequent mobilization to sites of economic construction. In a contrast, the individual battle ability of ROK troops is absolutely superior to that of the North, thanks to enhanced actual battle ability made possible by the use of high-tech equipment.

With regard to weapons systems and equipment performance, 20 percent of North Korean tanks and field guns have become superannuated and, besides, the calibre of its field guns highly varies, ranging from 76.2 mm to 240 mm, posing a difficulty in the supply of ammunition in an emergency. These inevitably weaken the battle ability of the DPRK military.

---

2. Source: *Chungang Ilbo*, Seoul, in Korean 2 October 1999 / BBC Monitoring / © BBC.

Of the DPRK's naval vessels, 15 percent are 20 years old or older, and 83 per cent are small ships of 200 or fewer tons, which limits their radius of operations. In fact, the materials said that the inferior battle ability was objectively proven in the Yonpyong sea battle of last 15th June.

In the DPRK air force, up-to-date models like MiG-23/29 and Su-25 account for a mere 30 percent of all planes, with the remainder being old models of the 1970s or earlier. In addition, the performance of such avionics as radar and navigational instruments lags far behind the ROK, posing many problems to all-weather air operations.

Moreover, the DPRK's economic ability is no more than a twenty-fifth of that of the ROK, making the DPRK absolutely inferior in terms of materials mobilization and its ability to continue a war. The DPRK further suffers from the collapse of its base of support from China and Russia, both one-time blood-tested allies of the DPRK. On the contrary, the ROK maintains thorough joint preparedness with the United States, the world's sole superpower.

The Troop Information and Publication Affairs Office, however, called for "strenuous efforts to prevent war through watertight defense preparedness," saying, "Victory in war would be meaningless because, if the DPRK were to use the some 4,000 tons of chemical weapons in its possession, more than 50 percent of the population in North and South Korea would die and more than 80 percent of the national land would be devastated."

Facts About Armed Forces on Peninsula*

THE KOREA HERALD, JUNE 7, 2003

USFK: There are 37,489 American troops in South Korea, including 28,300 Army soldiers, 8,706 Air Force personnel, 400 sailors and 83 Marines.

The 8th U.S. Army in South Korea has 140 M1A1 Abrams tanks, 30 155mm self-propelled howitzers, 30 multiple rocket launchers, and 70 AH-64 Apache helicopters. The 7th U.S. Air Force in South Korea possesses 70 F-16 fighter jets, 20 A-10 anti-tank attack planes, and U-2 and other reconnaissance planes.

South Korea: The army has 11 corps, 49 divisions, and 19 brigades, with a total of 560,000 troops. It has 2,360 tanks, 5,180 pieces of field artillery, and 2,400 armored vehicles.

The navy has 67,000 sailors and marines, 190 warships and transport vessels, as well as several submarines. In April, it launched its second stealth destroyer capable of spying electronically on North Korea.

The air force has 63,000 troops and 800 aircraft, including 100 F-16 fighters. It plans to build 40 F-15 fighter jets by 2009.

North Korea: North Korea's armed forces have 1.1 million soldiers, two-thirds of them deployed near the border with South Korea. The North

---

* Reprinted with permission of The Associated Press.

has many multiple launchers that could shower thousands of artillery rounds over Seoul, the South Korean capital.

Its army has 3,400 tanks, most of them old Soviet T-54/55/59s. In recent years, it has domestically produced T-62 tanks. The navy possesses 750 warships, 22 Romeo-class submarines and 60 midget submarines.

The air force has 590 aircraft, most of them made in China and the former Soviet Union, including MiG-19s, 21s and 23s. In the early 1990s, North Korea began assembling MiG-29s with Russian technological support. North Korea produces and exports Scud missiles. It has deployed Rodong-1 missiles with a range of 1,300 kilometers (810 miles) since 1997. It is believed to be developing Taepodong missiles that can reach part of northeast America.

North Korea is also suspected of developing nuclear weapons.

Nuclear Nightmare[3]

By Lou Dobbs
U.S. News & World Report, May 5, 2003

The crisis on the Korean peninsula is escalating at a frightening speed, even as talks to defuse the crisis have begun, if fitfully. And the threat of the tyrannical Kim Jong Il in North Korea and his nuclear weapons arsenal could have a devastating effect on the geopolitics and economics of that region and, perhaps, the world.

An explosive combination of factors is now in play in Pyongyang, including a cruel despot, an economy in ruins, and a nuclear weapons program that North Korean officials have threatened to accelerate. North Korea's per capita gross domestic product was an estimated $1,000 last year.

That's compared with $19,000 in South Korea, which has twice the population of North Korea. As many as 2 million North Koreans are thought to have died from starvation since the mid-'90s. And 42 percent of children in North Korea are chronically malnourished.

But while the North Korean economy implodes, its government continues to pour resources into its military. "North Korea has the fifth-largest standing army in the world with 1.1 million men in arms," says Chung Min Lee, professor at Yonsei University in Seoul. "It has over 700 ballistic missiles that target everything in South Korea and parts of Japan." And we now know that those missiles could reach the West Coast of the United States. Lee adds that North Korea also has a very large stockpile of biological and chemical weapons. North Korea has admitted to having at least one nuclear bomb, senior Bush administration sources have told CNN, and could soon be adding to its nuclear arsenal. Recently, it restarted a plutonium-based nuclear reactor at Yongbyon, which can be used to create the fuel for nuclear bombs. And in the past two weeks, North Korea has acknowledged it is moving forward with plans to reprocess that fuel. Robert Gallucci, former assistant secretary of state in the Clinton administration, says "whether it's in six months or in 12 months," North Korea will have enough material for five or six weapons.

Pressure politics. Compounding the problem, North Korea has already passed significant ballistic missile technology on to Iran, Pakistan, and Syria—a terrifying precedent for a country with nuclear weapons, an economy on the brink, and a starving population. That level of risk is understandably unacceptable to the

---

United States and, we would hope, the world. Last week, the United States, North Korea, and China met in Beijing for initial talks to resolve the issues. The discussions follow months of wrangling between Washington and Pyongyang over whether the talks should be one on one or multilateral. But even with a preliminary dialogue underway, the options to bring North Korea back under control are complex and limited. "We can negotiate. We can pressure them. Or we can move to try to make them collapse," says Eric Heginbotham of the Council on Foreign Relations.

"The leverage, obviously, has to be both negative and positive," says former National Security Adviser Zbigniew Brzezinski. "The negative leverage is the threat, for example, of a regional boycott . . . of eventually even a regional embargo on North Korea and, as a last resort, even military action. But to achieve that you have to have a great deal of political consensus, and that's very difficult to manufacture." He adds that the positive inducements are some form of economic assistance but cautions "that may not be enough at this stage to get the North Koreans to roll back what they're already doing. They may be willing to slow down or to stop, but to have them really dismantle what they have been doing is going to take a lot of pressure."

The United States has already cut back our foreign aid, as have Japan and the European Union, according to Nicholas Eberstadt of the American Enterprise Institute. "The other two actors who have to be encouraged are South Korea and China . . . and there's much less political support for aid to North Korea than there was a year ago in South Korea—and that leaves China as the question mark." And what a big question mark it is. China is North Korea's No. 1 trading partner, and Eberstadt estimates that China provides as much as $470 million in aid to North Korea. If international pressures do not succeed in forcing a change in regime or policies and conduct, says Eberstadt, then "at the end of the road, there are unpleasant military options that would have to be discussed."

Concerns about conflict in the region are already pressuring regional economies. Debt-rating agency Moody's has downgraded South Korea to "negative"—a move that Heginbotham says "got South Korea to start re-examining their North Korea policy much more than the nuclear crisis itself." Brzezinski says that in the past, North Korea couldn't use nuclear weapons offensively because it would have nothing left. "But once they have several," he warns, "then they are in a much better position to exercise choice, even to exert blackmail."

A Balance of Terror[4]

By Thomas Omestad et al.
U.S. News & World Report, January 27, 2003

It is a scenario that some U.S. officials find too sensitive to discuss in detail: A defiant North Korea chooses to build and keep a nuclear arsenal, not bargain it away for rewards, as many suppose. Faced with a nuclear breakout by a hostile regime, Japan reconsiders its antinuclear taboos, fields a larger missile force of its own, and plunges into developing a shield against incoming missiles with the United States. South Korea, with one eye on the North and the other on Japan, follows suit. China reacts with more nukes and missiles of its own. Taiwan, outgunned, opts for more missiles and, perhaps, nuclear bombs. A nervous Russia shifts nuclear and conventional forces for defense against its old rivals, China and Japan. India, a foe of China, expands its nuclear forces, a step that causes Pakistan to do likewise. An Asian arms race snaps into high gear. No wonder that one former U.S. official who helped guide North Korea policy warns of a new "domino effect" in Asia.

Such possibilities—even if only partially realized—are driving some U.S. officials and Asia specialists to conclude that Pyongyang's nuclear gambit could be the most serious threat to global stability today. In just over three months, North Korea has admitted running a covert program to enrich uranium for bombs, vowed to keep it going, and bustled through measures to prepare for extracting weapons-grade plutonium at another site. What's more, it became the first nation to abandon the Nuclear Nonproliferation Treaty—and declared that it would cast off a moratorium on test-firing ballistic missiles.

That may not be an idle threat. A senior State Department official predicted last week that the North may soon test-fire a long-range missile over Japan, as it did in 1998. The dizzying pace of North Korea's brinkmanship is deepening suspicions that its leader, Kim Jong Il, has made the strategic choice to build a nuclear arsenal in order to deter any potential U.S. attack. Says Victor Cha, a North Korea expert at Georgetown University, "If you're simply trying to create a crisis, you don't need to do all these things."

Options. Kim's actions, note U.S. officials, seem designed to expand his options. He could build up a nuclear arsenal in a bid to win greater concessions through security guarantees, aid, and diplomatic recognition. Or he could keep it as a deterrent force. He

---

The North Korean Threat

U.S. intelligence agencies believe that North Korea has "one, possibly two" nuclear weapons. It agreed to freeze its nuclear-weapons program in a 1994 deal with the United States but is now preparing to resume those activities. If unchecked, experts say, North Korea could produce five to seven nuclear bombs this year—and eight to 10 by the end of 2005—enough to alter the strategic balance in East Asia. North Korea is probably capable of deploying nuclear or chemical warheads on ballistic missiles able to strike South Korea and Japan, and it has worked on the Taepo Dong-2 missile, which has an estimated range that could include part of Alaska.

Under the Gun
North Korea's current midrange ballistic missiles, No Dong and Taepo Dong-1, could carry chemical or nuclear warheads against South Korea, Japan, Russia, and China.

Taepo Dong-2
In development. The estimated 2,500 to 3,700-mile range could enable it to strike Alaska.

---

might try to do both by hiding a portion of any newly produced fissile material. And having seen India and Pakistan ride out sanctions after their 1998 nuclear tests, Kim may be calculating that he can do likewise.

In a few weeks, the North could begin lifting some of the 8,000 plutonium fuel rods from a cooling pool at the Yongbyon reactor complex for reprocessing. That could yield enough weapons-grade plutonium for five to seven bombs by this summer—on top of the one or two nuclear devices the North may have already. By then, the North would be in a position to consider a dramatic act of brinkmanship: a nuclear test blast. Says a high-ranking State Department official, "If they test and reprocess furiously, it's a monumental change. Everyone in the region has to reassess their defenses."

Some Russian and Chinese military analysts doubt that the North Koreans have been able to make workable weapons. U.S. proliferation specialists, however, believe that the North has conducted dozens of test explosions of the sort that can touch off a chain reaction in plutonium.

Selling nukes. A half-dozen nukes would make Asia a different place. "It's a much more threatening capability," says Robert Einhorn, a former top U.S. nonproliferation official. The weapons could be dispersed—and hidden in underground bunkers. And North Korea's track record of selling missiles to countries such as Pakistan and Yemen raises an even more chilling prospect: the world's first department store for nukes, with terrorists and rogue states as potential hard-currency customers. One senior U.S. official doubts Kim would go that far: "I think he knows we would cause him to disappear."

The Two Koreas

	North	South
Population:	22.2 million	48.3 million*
GDP:	$21.8 billion*	$865 billion*
GDP per capita:	$1,000*	$18,000*

Figures are estimates

*Adjusted for purchasing-power differences

The Bush administration has been trying to orchestrate international pressure on the North to disarm—with limited success. In a shift last week, the president softened his rhetoric, hinting that impoverished North Korea might receive aid, energy supplies, and even agreements on security and diplomatic recognition if it verifiably quits its nuclear projects. South Korea's incoming president, Roh Moo Hyun, has frustrated administration hawks by portraying himself as a possible mediator between Pyongyang and Washington, and Seoul opposes sanctions or other efforts to isolate the North. Russia, which has friendly ties with the North, remains stuck in a "denial phase" on Pyongyang's nuclear ambitions, says Alexander Vershbow, the U.S. ambassador to Moscow.

China may be the key: North Korea depends on China for food and fuel, but Beijing has been reluctant to squeeze Pyongyang, fearing chaos, mass refugee flows, and a U.S. presence on its border if the North collapses. U.S. officials welcomed China's offer last week to host U.S.–North Korean talks, but they hope for more. Envoys are reminding the Chinese that Washington has opposed a nuclear-armed Japan or South Korea. "We say, 'We've carried your water on nuclear issues for 50 years. Now it's your turn to do it for us,'" says a senior U.S. diplomat.

Japan has edged closer to the U.S. approach than has South Korea. The Japanese public was enraged by revelations last fall of North Korean abductions of Japanese. Normalization talks have stalled. After the nuclear crisis emerged, officials in Tokyo approached the Bush administration about increasing Japan's role in theater missile defenses. The revulsion at atomic weapons is deep in Japan, the only country to have suffered a nuclear attack. But the idea that Japan someday might have to abandon its non-nuclear stance has also gained currency in conservative circles. If Pyongyang brandishes atomic weapons, says Ryukichi Imai, a former diplomat and government adviser on atomic energy, "there would be a lot of voices in Japan saying this country should do it too." But, he predicts, "Japan will never have the bomb. We know too much about nuclear weapons." Still, U.S. officials note

Approximate Maximum Ranges of
North Korean Missiles

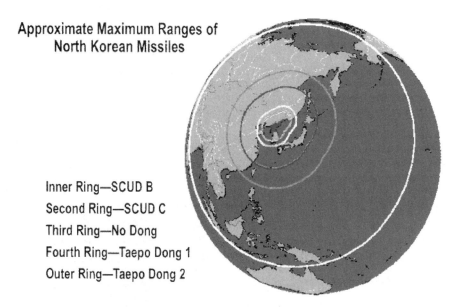

Inner Ring—SCUD B

Second Ring—SCUD C

Third Ring—No Dong

Fourth Ring—Taepo Dong 1

Outer Ring—Taepo Dong 2

Source: Perrt-Castaneda Library Map Collection

that Japan has plenty of plutonium and technical know-how. "Japan in six to 12 months could be missiled and weaponed up," says a senior U.S. official.

Banned the bomb. South Korea has also shunned the bomb, though it conducted covert nuclear weapons research in the 1970s until the United States leaned on Seoul to shut it down. "They were close," says the U.S. official. "The plans are on the shelf." (Washington also demanded that Taiwan halt its nuclear research around the same time.) Though analysts believe the South might react to a prolonged nuclear crisis by acquiring antimissile systems and perhaps offensive missiles, the Seoul government insists the nuclear question is closed. "South Korea knows it can be safely protected behind the U.S. military. The U.S. [nuclear] umbrella is sufficient," says a senior official in Seoul.

South Korea is also defended by a "tripwire" 37,000-member U.S. military force. Yet even before the current tensions, *U.S. News* has learned, the Pentagon was studying a possible reduction in the ground force, which has been a magnet for anti-American protests in the South, coupled with other changes including greater emphasis on Navy and Air Force precision-strike weapons. Those moves, however, could be complicated by the nuclear crisis if U.S. officials believe that North Korea would interpret them as a weakening of the U.S. commitment to defending the South.

But in Seoul, some people already believe that American nuclear protection isn't enough. "If South Korea has nuclear weapons, then South Korea will never fear North Korea, because it will know that if North Korea bombs South Korea, it will be bombed by us," reasons Kim Young Tak, a 43-year-old middle school teacher. Nuclear deterrence, it's been said, has an undeniable logic.

Military Might			
China		**North Korea**	
Nuclear warheads	410	Nuclear warheads	1 or 2
Military forces	2.3 million	Military forces	1.08 million
Russia		**South Korea**	
Nuclear warheads	20,000	Nuclear warheads	0
Military forces	1 million	Military forces	683,000
Japan		U.S. troops in S. Korea	37,000
Nuclear warheads	0	**United States**	
Military forces	239,800	Nuclear warheads	10,700
U.S. troops in Japan	38,330	Military forces	1.4 million

Talks on North Korea Nuclear Program End[5]

THE ASSOCIATED PRESS, FEBRUARY 28, 2004

Six-nation talks on ending North Korea's alleged nuclear weapons program made more progress than expected, a top U.S. delegate said Saturday as the meeting ended. Pyongyang said it would never give up its peaceful nuclear program.

The meeting ended with agreement to hold more negotiations before July and form a lower-level "working group" to handle details of the 16-month-old dispute. Both are steps toward establishing an enduring line of communication between the United States and the North, which have no diplomatic relations.

The communist North, however, gave no ground on U.S. demands that it completely give up its nuclear ambitions and insisted on keeping technology and equipment used to generate electricity, among other "peaceful purposes."

"We don't plan to include our civilian nuclear program, for peaceful purposes, in the freeze and dismantlement," said the North's chief delegate, Vice Foreign Minister Kim Kye Gwan.

Washington claims North Korea has admitted producing a nuclear bomb, an allegation the North denies.

A senior U.S. official said he was upbeat after four days of talks and sometimes confusing signals but said the U.S. goal of a nuclear-free North Korea had not changed.

But the U.S. official, who spoke to The Associated Press on condition of anonymity, said: "I'm not aware of any peaceful nuclear programs in the DPRK, so this is an issue that will have to be dealt with over time."

Participants said they expected a long process ahead over key contentious issues, including how deeply the North would be willing to cut its nuclear development. So far it is offering only to freeze and dismantle what it terms its "nuclear weapons program."

The second round of talks, held six months after meetings in August made no progress, brought together the Koreas, the United States, Russia, China, and Japan to hash out whether the Korean Peninsula can be made free of nuclear weapons.

All parties—including the North—say they want that, but their definitions of "nuclear-free" have varied.

---

5. Reprinted with permission of The Associated Press.

1999 Map of North Korea's Nuclear Program

Map from the Center for Nonproliferation Studies Web site, *cns.miis.edu.*
Copyright © Center for Nonproliferation Studies, Monterey Institute of International Studies.
Reprinted with permission.

"Differences" Remain

Despite the upbeat U.S. assessment, the four days of negotiations, more intense and lengthier than the last round, ended on a discordant note.

On Saturday, after the closing ceremony was delayed for three hours, the governments failed to issue their planned joint statement because of North Korea's last-minute request to change the wording. It wanted to refer to "differences" among participants, diplomats said.

Even after the ceremony was scheduled, every delegation but North Korea's sat waiting for several tense minutes—broadcast live on Chinese television—as the sixth side of the table remained empty. Finally, Kim and his entourage strode in and took their seats.

Hours later, the revised document emerged as an unsigned "chairman's statement" that emphasized progress and cooperation, but the deep divides that fuel the dispute were clear.

"The main reason for these differences is the extreme lack of trust," said China's delegation chief, Vice Foreign Minister Wang Yi.

Kim said in a rare news conference at his country's embassy that the talks saw no "positive result," a complaint for which he blamed the United States.

"The big achievement of the talks is that we clearly learned there are great differences between participating countries, especially between North Korea and the United States," Kim said.

He said his delegation offered to freeze its nuclear-weapons activities and dismantle the program if the United States drops its "hostile policy." North Korea has been demanding security guarantees, free oil, and other aid from the United States in exchange for action.

During the talks, South Korea, China, and Russia offered the North crucial energy aid if it agreed to disarm. Washington said it "understands" the offer but declined to sign on; it has repeatedly ruled out any concession before Pyongyang "completely, verifiably, and irreversibly dismantles" all nuclear programs.

The United States affirmed Saturday that it had "no hostile intent" against the North, Wang said—a major concern of Pyongyang's, particularly since President Bush included the North in an "axis of evil" in 2002.

The United States "has no intention to invade or attack North Korea," Wang said. "It has no intention to seek regime change."

U.S., N. Korea Still at Odds

The delegates had met since Wednesday in the Chinese capital for the second round of six-party talks, a gathering that took months to put together. The last set, in August, produced some discord but no substantive result.

North Korea and the United States have been at odds over Pyongyang's nuclear ambitions for years and specially since October 2002, when U.S. Assistant Secretary of State James Kelly said the North told him it had a secret program based on enriched uranium—thus, Washington said, violating a 1994 agreement. Kelly led the U.S. delegation to the Beijing talks.

Another sticking point is American allegations that the North has a uranium program besides its known plutonium-based program, a charge the North has loudly denied. But it brandishes the threat of what it describes as its "nuclear deterrent" to extract concessions.

U.S. officials believe North Korea already has one or two nuclear bombs and could make several more within months.

Timeline: Tension with North Korea

1993
North Korea quits the Nuclear Nonproliferation Treaty amid suspicions that it is developing nuclear weapons.

1994
North Korea and United States sign nuclear agreement in Geneva. Under the Agreed Framework, North Korea pledges to freeze and eventually dismantle its nuclear weapons program in exchange for international aid to build two power-producing nuclear reactors, worth $4.6 billion, and interim fuel supplies.

Aug. 31, 1998
North Korea fires a multistage rocket that flies over Japan and lands in the Pacific Ocean, proving Pyongyang can strike any part of Japan.

Nov. 17
The United States and North Korea hold the first round of high-level talks in Pyongyang over North Korea's suspected construction of an underground nuclear facility. The United States demands inspections.

Feb. 27–March 16, 1999
During a fourth round of talks, North Korea allows U.S. access to the site in exchange for promises of food. U.S. inspectors find no evidence of any nuclear activity during visit to site in May.

May 25–28
Former Defense Secretary William Perry visits North Korea and delivers a U.S. disarmament proposal during four days of talks.

September
North Korea pledges to freeze testing of long-range missiles for the duration of negotiations to improve relations. President Clinton agrees to the first significant easing of economic sanctions against North Korea since the Korean War ended in 1953.

July 2000
North Korea renews its threat to restart its nuclear program if Washington does not compensate for the loss of electricity caused by delays in building nuclear power plants.

November
President George W. Bush is elected after vowing during his campaign to review the U.S. policy of engagement with North Korea that had been pursued during the Clinton administration.

June 2001
North Korea warns it will reconsider its moratorium on missile tests if the Bush administration doesn't resume contacts aimed at normalizing relations.

July
State Department reports North Korea is going ahead with development of its long-range missile. A senior Bush administration official says North Korea has conducted an engine test of the Taepodong-1 missile.

December
As the war on terrorism gets into full swing following the Sept. 11 attacks on the United States, President Bush warns Iraq and North Korea that they will be "held accountable" if they develop weapons of mass destruction "that will be used to terrorize nations."

Jan. 29, 2002
Bush labels North Korea, Iran and Iraq an "axis of evil" in his State of the Union address. "By seeking weapons of mass destruction, these regimes pose a grave and growing danger," he says.

April 6
North Korea agrees to revive stalled dialogue with Washington and South Korea and says it

is willing to hold talks with a U.S. envoy.

Sept. 25
President Bush plans to send an envoy to North Korea, reopening security talks with the country for the first time in almost two years.

Oct. 16
A U.S. official reveals that North Korea has admitted to a secret uranium enrichment program, which Washington says violates the 1994 agreement.

November
The Bush administration announces suspension of fuel oil shipments to North Korea, provided under the 1994 Agreed Framework.

Dec. 21
The International Atomic Energy Agency says North Korea has interfered with its safeguards and surveillance equipment at a nuclear complex and accuses North Korea of "nuclear brinkmanship."

Dec. 31
IAEA inspectors are expelled from North Korea.

Jan. 10–11, 2003
North Korea announces its withdrawal from the Nuclear Nonproliferation Treaty (NPT) but says it has no intention of developing nuclear weapons. Its withdrawal from the treaty becomes official the next day. The North's envoy to China suggests Pyongyang is free to resume missile tests.

Jan. 12–13
Undersecretary of State James Kelly holds talks in South Korea and holds out the promise of aid if Pyongyang takes steps to defuse the crisis.

Feb. 6
North Korea says it has reactivated its nuclear facilities.

Feb. 12
IAEA holds emergency meeting, refers standoff to the U.N. Security Council.

April 23–24
U.S. and North Korean envoys hold talks in Beijing, organized by the Chinese, in an effort to resolve the standoff over the North's nuclear program. North Korea privately tells U.S. officials that it has nuclear weapons and may test, export or use them depending on U.S. actions. Pyongyang says it also proposed a plan to end the standoff, offering to give up its nuclear program in exchange for aid.

May 12
North Korea withdraws from a 1992 agreement with South Korea to keep the Korean Peninsula free of nuclear weapons.

Aug. 1
North Korea says it has agreed to take part in six-nation talks on its nuclear program, reversing earlier insistence that it would talk only with the United States alone about the issue.

Aug. 27–29
North Korea, the United States, China, South Korea, Japan and Russia meet in Beijing for talks aimed at resolving the tensions surrounding Pyongyang's nuclear ambitions. The talks are inconclusive except for an agreement to meet again in coming months. Pyongyang has since said it was not interested in continuing, but efforts continued to organize the talks.

Oct. 2–3
Pyongyang repeats a claim that it has reprocessed all 8,000 spent fuel rods at its Yongbyon nuclear facility, enough to build five or six nuclear weapons, and claims to have overcome technological hurdles to building nuclear weapons. Some observers see this as a negotiating strategy.

Source: The Associated Press

Appendix

Korean Peninsula

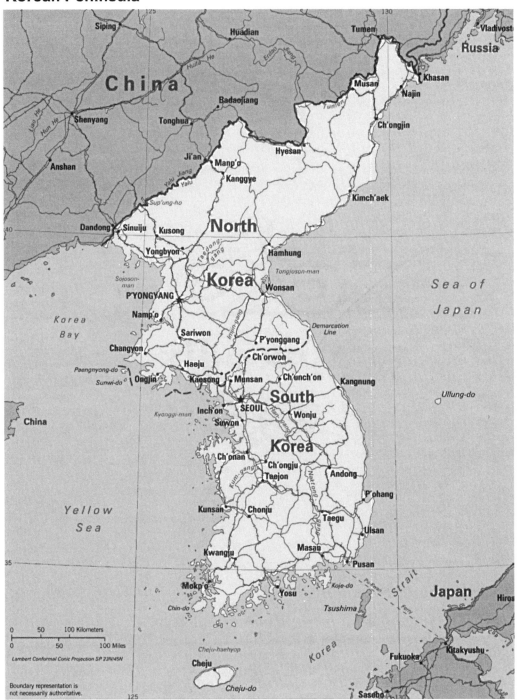

South Korea

From *The World Factbook 2003*, prepared by the Central Intelligence Agency of the United States, *www.cia.gov*.

Introduction

Background: After World War II, a republic was set up in the southern half of the Korean Peninsula while a Communist-style government was installed in the north. During the Korean War (1950–1953), U.S. and other U.N. forces intervened to defend South Korea from North Korean attacks supported by the Chinese. An armistice was signed in 1953, splitting the Peninsula along a demilitarized zone at about the 38th parallel. Thereafter, South Korea achieved rapid economic growth with per capita income rising to roughly 20 times the level of North Korea. South Korea has maintained its commitment to democratize its political processes. In June 2000, a historic first North-South summit took place between the South's President KIM Dae-jung and the North's leader KIM Jong-il.

Geography

Location: Eastern Asia, southern half of the Korean Peninsula bordering the Sea of Japan and the Yellow Sea

Geographic coordinates: 37' N, 127' 30" E

Map references: Asia

Area:
total: 98,480 sq km
land: 98,190 sq km
water: 290 sq km

Area—comparative: slightly larger than Indiana

Land boundaries:
total: 238 km
border countries: North Korea 238 km

Coastline: 2,413 km

Maritime claims:
contiguous zone: 24 NM
territorial sea: 12 NM; between 3 NM and 12 NM in the Korea Strait
continental shelf: not specified
exclusive economic zone: 200 NM

Climate: temperate, with rainfall heavier in summer than winter

Terrain: mostly hills and mountains; wide coastal plains in west and south

Elevation extremes:
> *lowest point*: Sea of Japan 0 m
> *highest point*: Halla-san 1,950 m

Natural resources: coal, tungsten, graphite, molybdenum, lead, hydropower potential

Land use:
> *arable land*: 17.44%
> *permanent crops*: 2.05%
> *other*: 80.51% (1998 est.)

Irrigated land: 11,590 sq km (1998 est.)

Natural hazards: occasional typhoons bring high winds and floods; low-level seismic activity common in southwest

Environment—current issues: air pollution in large cities; acid rain; water pollution from the discharge of sewage and industrial effluents; drift net fishing

Environment—international agreements:
> *party to*: Antarctic-Environmental Protocol, Antarctic-Marine Living Resources, Antarctic Treaty, Biodiversity, Climate Change, Desertification, Endangered Species, Environmental Modification, Hazardous Wastes, Law of the Sea, Marine Dumping, Nuclear Test Ban, Ozone Layer Protection, Ship Pollution, Tropical Timber 83, Tropical Timber 94, Wetlands, Whaling
> *signed, but not ratified*: Climate Change-Kyoto Protocol

Geography—note: strategic location on Korea Strait

People

Population: 48,289,037 (July 2003 est.)

Age structure:
> *0–14 years*: 20.6% (male 5,256,451; female 4,703,853)
> *15–64 years*: 71.5% (male 17,527,407; female 16,991,229)
> *65 years and over*: 7.9% (male 1,512,157; female 2,297,940) (2003 est.)

Median age:
> *total*: 33.2 years
> *male*: 32.2 years
> *female*: 34.2 years (2002)

Population growth rate: 0.66% (2003 est.)

Birth rate: 12.6 births/1,000 population (2003 est.)

Death rate: 6.03 deaths/1,000 population (2003 est.)

Net migration rate: 0 migrant(s)/1,000 population (2003 est.)

Sex ratio:
   at birth: 1.1 male(s)/female
   under 15 years: 1.12 male(s)/female
   15–64 years: 1.03 male(s)/female
   65 years and over: 0.66 male(s)/female
   total population: 1.01 male(s)/female (2003 est.)

Infant mortality rate:
   total: 7.31 deaths/1,000 live births
   female: 6.8 deaths/1,000 live births (2003 est.)
   male: 7.77 deaths/1,000 live births

Life expectancy at birth:
   total population: 75.36 years
   male: 71.73 years
   female: 79.32 years (2003 est.)

Total fertility rate: 1.56 children born/woman (2003 est.)

HIV/AIDS—adult prevalence rate: less than 0.1% (2001 est.)

HIV/AIDS—people living with HIV/AIDS: 4,000 (2001 est.)

HIV/AIDS—deaths: 220 (2001 est.)

Nationality:
   noun: Korean(s)
   adjective: Korean

Ethnic groups: homogeneous (except for about 20,000 Chinese)

Religions: Christian 49%, Buddhist 47%, Confucianist 3%, Shamanist, Chondogyo (Religion of the Heavenly Way), and other 1%

Languages: Korean, English widely taught in junior high and high school

Literacy:
   definition: age 15 and over can read and write
   total population: 98.1%
   male: 99.3%
   female: 97% (2003 est.)

Government

Country name:
   conventional long form: Republic of Korea
   conventional short form: South Korea
   local short form: none
   note: the South Koreans generally use the term "Han'guk" to refer to their country
   local long form: Taehan-min'guk
   abbreviation: ROK

Government type: republic

Capital: Seoul

Administrative divisions: 9 provinces (do, singular and plural) and 7 metropolitan cities* (gwangyoksi, singular and plural); Cheju-do, Cholla-bukto, Cholla-namdo, Ch'ungch'ong-bukto, Ch'ungch'ong-namdo, Inch'on-gwangyoksi*, Kangwon-do, Kwangju-gwangyoksi*, Kyonggi-do, Kyongsang-bukto, Kyongsang-namdo, Pusan-gwangyoksi*, Soul-t'ukpyolsi*, Taegu-gwangyoksi*, Taejon-gwangyoksi*, Ulsan-gwangyoksi*

Independence: 15 August 1945 (from Japan)

National holiday: Liberation Day, 15 August (1945)

Constitution: 17 July 1948

Legal system: combines elements of continental European civil law systems, Anglo-American law, and Chinese classical thought

Suffrage: 20 years of age; universal

Executive branch:
chief of state: President NO Mu-hyun (ROH Moo-hyun) (since 25 February 2003)

head of government: Prime Minister KO Kun (KOH Kun) (since 27 February 2003); Deputy Prime Ministers KIM Chin-p'yo (KIM Jin-pyo) (since 27 February 2003) and YUN Tok-hong (since 6 March 2003)

cabinet: State Council appointed by the president on the prime minister's recommendation

elections: president elected by popular vote for a single five-year term; election last held 19 December 2002 (next to be held NA December 2007); prime minister appointed by the president; deputy prime ministers appointed by the president on the prime minister's recommendation

election results: results of the 19 December 2002 election—NO Muh-hyun elected president, took office 25 February 2003; percent of vote—NO Muh-hyun (MDP) 48.9%; YI Hoe-ch'ang (GNP) 46.6%; other 4.5%

Legislative branch: unicameral National Assembly or Kukhoe (273 seats total—227 elected by direct, popular vote; members serve four-year terms); note—beginning in 2004, all members will be directly elected; possible redistricting before 2004 may affect the number of seats in the National Assembly.

elections: last held 13 April 2000 (next to be held NA April 2004)

election results: percent of vote by party—NA%; seats by party—GNP 133, MDP 115, ULD 17, other 8; note—the distribution of seats as of April 2003 was: GNP 153, MDP 101, ULD 11, DPP 1, PPR 1, independents 5; one seat vacant.

Judicial branch: Supreme Court (justices are appointed by the president with the consent of the National Assembly)

Political parties and leaders: Democratic People's Party or DPP [leader NA]; Grand National Party or GNP [CH'OE Pyong-ryol, chairman]; Millennium Democratic Party or MDP [CHO Sun-hyong, chairman]; United Liberal Democrats or ULD [KIM Chong-p'il, president]; Uri Party [KIM Kun-t'ae, chairman]

Political pressure groups and leaders: Federation of Korean Industries; Federation of Korean Trade Unions; Korean Confederation of Trade Unions; Korean National Council of Churches; Korean Traders Association; Korean Veterans' Association; National Council of Labor Unions; National Democratic Alliance of Korea; National Federation of Farmers' Associations; National Federation of Student Associations

International organization participation: AfDB, APEC, ARF (dialogue partner), AsDB, ASEAN (dialogue partner), Australia Group, BIS, CP, EBRD, ESCAP, FAO, IAEA, IBRD, ICAO, ICC, ICCt, ICFTU, ICRM, IDA, IEA, IEA (observer), IFAD, IFC, IFRCS, IHO, ILO, IMF, IMO, Interpol, IOC, IOM, ISO, ITU, MINURSO, NAM (guest), NEA, NSG, OAS (observer), OECD, OPCW, OSCE (partner), PCA, UN, UNCTAD, UNESCO, UNFICYP, UNHCR, UNIDO, UNMISET, UNMOGIP, UNOMIG, UNU, UPU, WCL, WCO, WHO, WIPO, WMO, WToO, WTrO, ZC

Diplomatic representation in the U.S.:

chief of mission: Ambassador HAN Sung-chu (HAN Sung-joo)
consulate(s): New York, Tamuning (Guam)
consulate(s) general: Atlanta, Boston, Chicago, Honolulu, Houston, Los Angeles, New York, San Francisco, and Seattle
FAX: [1] (202) 387-0205
telephone: [1] (202) 939-5600
chancery: 2450 Massachusetts Avenue NW, Washington, DC 20008

Diplomatic representation from the U.S.:

chief of mission: Ambassador Thomas C. HUBBARD
embassy: 82 Sejong-no, Jongno-gu, Seoul 110-710
mailing address: American Embassy, Unit 15550, APO AP 96205-5550
telephone: [82] (2) 397-4114
FAX: [82] (2) 738-8845

Flag description: white with a red (top) and blue yin-yang symbol in the center; there is a different black trigram from the ancient I Ching (Book of Changes) in each corner of the white field

Economy

Overview: As one of the Four Tigers of East Asia, South Korea has achieved an incredible record of growth and integration into the high-tech modern world economy. Three decades ago GDP per capita was comparable with levels in the poorer countries of Africa and Asia. Today its GDP per capita is 18 times North Korea's and equal to the lesser economies of the European Union. This success through the late 1980s was achieved by a system of close government/business ties, including directed credit, import restrictions, sponsorship of specific industries, and a strong labor effort. The government promoted the import of raw materials and technology at the expense of consumer goods and encouraged savings and investment over consumption. The Asian financial crisis of 1997–99 exposed longstanding weaknesses in South Korea's development model, including high debt/equity ratios, massive foreign borrowing, and an undisciplined financial sector. Growth plunged to a negative 6.6% in 1998, then strongly recovered to 10.8% in 1999 and 9.2% in 2000. Growth fell back to 3.3% in 2001 because of the slowing global economy, falling exports, and the perception that much-needed corporate and financial reforms had stalled. Led by consumer spending and exports, growth in 2002 was an impressive 6.2%, despite anemic global growth, followed by moderate 2.8% growth in 2003. In 2003 the six-day work week was reduced to five days.

GDP: purchasing power parity—$941.5 billion (2002 est.)

GDP—real growth rate: 6.3% (2002 est.)

GDP—per capita: purchasing power parity—$19,600 (2002 est.)

GDP—composition by sector:
  agriculture: 4.4%
  industry: 41.6%
  services: 54% (2001 est.)

Population below poverty line: 4% (2001 est.)

Household income or consumption by percentage share:
  lowest 10%: 2.6%
  highest 10%: 24.8% (1998 est.)

Distribution of family income—Gini index: 31.6 (1993)

Inflation rate (consumer prices): 2.8% (2002 est.)

Labor force: 22 million (2001)

Labor force—by occupation: services 69%, industry 21.5%, agriculture 9.5% (2001)

Unemployment rate: 3.1% (2002 est.)

Budget:
  revenues: $118.1 billion
  expenditures: $95.7 billion, including capital expenditures of $22.6 billion (2000)

Industries: electronics, automobile production, chemicals, shipbuilding, steel, textiles, clothing, footwear, food processing

Industrial production growth rate: 6.5% (2002 est.)

Electricity—production: 290.7 billion kWh (2001)

Electricity—production by source:
  fossil fuel: 62.4%
  hydro: 0.8%
  other: 0.2% (2001)
  nuclear: 36.6%

Electricity—consumption: 270.3 billion kWh (2001)

Electricity—exports: 0 kWh (2001)

Electricity—imports: 0 kWh (2001)

Oil—production: 0 bbl/day (2001 est.)

Oil—consumption: 2.14 million bbl/day (2001 est.)

Oil—exports: 804,700 bbl/day (2001)

Oil—imports: 2.965 million bbl/day (2001)

Natural gas—production: 0 cu m (2001 est.)

Natural gas—consumption: 20.92 billion cu m (2001 est.)

Natural gas—exports: 0 cu m (2001 est.)

Natural gas—imports: 21.11 billion cu m (2001 est.)

Agriculture—products: rice, root crops, barley, vegetables, fruit; cattle, pigs, chickens, milk, eggs; fish

Exports: $162.6 billion f.o.b. (2002 est.)

Exports—commodities: electronic products, machinery and equipment, motor vehicles, steel, ships; textiles, clothing, footwear; fish

Exports—partners: U.S. 20.4%, China 14.7%, Japan 9.4%, Hong Kong 6.3% (2002)

Imports: $148.4 billion f.o.b. (2002 est.)

Imports—commodities: machinery, electronics and electronic equipment, oil, steel, transport equipment, textiles, organic chemicals, grains

Imports—partners: Japan 19.6%, U.S. 15.2%, China 11.4%, Saudi Arabia 5% (2002)

Debt—external: $135.2 billion (year-end 2002 est.)

Economic aid—donor: ODA $200 million

Currency: South Korean won (KRW)

Currency code: KRW

Exchange rates: South Korean won per U.S. dollar—1,251.09 (2002), 1,290.99 (2001), 1,130.96 (2000), 1,188.82 (1999), 1,401.44 (1998)

Fiscal year: calendar year

Communications

Telephones—main lines in use: 24 million (2000)

Telephones—mobile cellular: 28 million (September 2000)

Telephone system:
general assessment: excellent domestic and international services
domestic: NA
international: fiber-optic   submarine   cable   to   China;   the   Rus-
sia-Korea-Japan submarine cable; satellite earth stations—3 Intelsat (2
Pacific Ocean and 1 Indian Ocean) and 1 Inmarsat (Pacific Ocean
region)

Radio broadcast stations: AM 104, FM 136, shortwave 5 (2001)

Radios: 47.5 million (2000)

Television broadcast stations: 121 (plus 850 repeater stations and the
eight-channel American Forces Korea Network) (1999)

Televisions: 15.9 million (1997)

Internet country code: .kr

Internet Service Providers (ISPs): 11 (2000)

Internet users: 25.6 million (2002)

Transportation

Railways:
total: 3,125 km
standard gauge: 3,125 km 1.435-m gauge (661 km electrified) (2002)

Highways:
total: 86,990 km
paved: 64,808 km (including 1,996 km of expressways)
unpaved: 22,182 km (1999 est.)

Waterways: 1,609 km
note: restricted to small native craft

Pipelines: gas 1,433 km; refined products 827 km (2003)

Ports and harbors: Chinhae, Inch'on, Kunsan, Masan, Mokp'o, P'ohang,
Pusan, Tonghae-hang, Ulsan, Yosu

Merchant marine:
total: 541 ships (1,000 GRT or over) 6,490,521 GRT/10,602,751 DWT
note: includes some foreign-owned ships registered here as a flag of convenience: Australia 1, Bulgaria 1, China 1, Greece 1, Japan 1, Malaysia 1,
Norway 1, Panama 1, Saint Vincent and the Grenadines 1, U.K. 1 (2002
est.)

ships by type: bulk 114, cargo 174, chemical tanker 63, combination bulk 9, container 52, liquefied gas 17, passenger 3, petroleum tanker 69, refrigerated cargo 21, roll on/roll off 6, short-sea passenger 2, specialized tanker 6, vehicle carrier 5

Airports: 102 (2002)

Airports—with paved runways:
total: 69
over 3,047 m: 3
2,438 to 3,047 m: 18
914 to 1,523 m: 11
under 914 m: 21 (2002)
1,524 to 2,437 m: 16

Airports—with unpaved runways:
total: 33
914 to 1,523 m: 2
under 914 m: 31 (2002)

Heliports: 204 (2002)

Military

Military branches: Army, Navy, Air Force, Marine Corps, National Maritime Police (Coast Guard)

Military manpower—military age: 18 years of age (2003 est.)

Military manpower—availability: males age 15–49: 14,252,851 (2003 est.)

Military manpower—fit for military service: males age 15–49: 8,994,941 (2003 est.)

Military manpower—reaching military age annually: males: 345,331 (2003 est.)

Military expenditures—dollar figure: $13,094.3 million (FY02)

Military expenditures—percent of GDP: 2.8% (FY02)

Transnational Issues

Disputes—international: Military Demarcation Line within the 4-km wide Demilitarized Zone has separated North from South Korea since 1953; Liancourt Rocks (Take-shima/Tok-do) are disputed with Japan.

North Korea

Introduction

Background: Following World War II, Korea was split, with the northern half coming under Communist domination and the southern portion becoming Western-oriented. KIM Jong-il has ruled North Korea since his father and the country's founder, president KIM Il-sung, died in 1994. After decades of mismanagement, the North relies heavily on international food aid to feed its population while continuing to expend resources to maintain an army of about 1 million. North Korea's long-range missile development and research into nuclear, chemical, and biological weapons and massive conventional armed forces are of major concern to the international community. In December 2002, North Korea repudiated a 1994 agreement that shut down its nuclear reactors and expelled U.N. monitors, further raising fears it would produce nuclear weapons.

Geography

Location: Eastern Asia, northern half of the Korean Peninsula bordering the Korea Bay and the Sea of Japan, between China and South Korea

Geographic coordinates: 40' N, 127' E

Map references: Asia

Area:
total: 120,540 sq km
water: 130 sq km
land: 120,410 sq km

Area—comparative: slightly smaller than Mississippi

Land boundaries:
total: 1,673 km
border countries: China 1,416 km, South Korea 238 km, Russia 19 km

Coastline: 2,495 km

Maritime claims:
territorial sea: 12 NM
exclusive economic zone: 200 NM
note: military boundary line 50 NM in the Sea of Japan and the exclusive economic zone limit in the Yellow Sea where all foreign vessels and aircraft without permission are banned

Climate: temperate with rainfall concentrated in summer

Terrain: mostly hills and mountains separated by deep, narrow valleys; coastal plains wide in west, discontinuous in east

Elevation extremes:
  lowest point: Sea of Japan 0 m
  highest point: Paektu-san 2,744 m

Natural resources: coal, lead, tungsten, zinc, graphite, magnesite, iron ore, copper, gold, pyrites, salt, fluorspar, hydropower

Land use:
  arable land: 14.12%
  permanent crops: 2.49%
  other: 83.39% (1998 est.)

Irrigated land: 14,600 sq km (1998 est.)

Natural hazards: late spring droughts often followed by severe flooding; occasional typhoons during the early fall

Environment—current issues: water pollution; inadequate supplies of potable water; water-borne disease; deforestation; soil erosion and degradation

Environment—international agreements:
  party to: Antarctic Treaty, Biodiversity, Climate Change, Environmental Modification, Ozone Layer Protection, Ship Pollution
  signed, but not ratified: Antarctic-Environmental Protocol, Law of the Sea

Geography—note: strategic location bordering China, South Korea, and Russia; mountainous interior is isolated and sparsely populated

People

Population: 22,466,481 (July 2003 est.)

Age structure:
  0–14 years: 25% (male 2,845,727; female 2,763,800)
  15–64 years: 67.8% (male 7,485,310; female 7,746,603)
  65 years and over: 7.2% (male 541,155; female 1,083,886) (2003 est.)

Median age:
  total: 31.1 years
  male: 30 years
  female: 32.3 years (2002)

Population growth rate: 1.07% (2003 est.)

Birth rate: 17.61 births/1,000 population (2003 est.)

Death rate: 6.93 deaths/1,000 population (2003 est.)

Net migration rate: 0 migrant(s)/1,000 population (2003 est.)

Sex ratio:
  at birth: 1.05 male(s)/female

under 15 years: 1.03 male(s)/female
15–64 years: 0.97 male(s)/female
65 years and over: 0.5 male(s)/female
total population: 0.94 male(s)/female (2003 est.)

Infant mortality rate:
   total: 25.66 deaths/1,000 live births
   female: 23.79 deaths/1,000 live births (2003 est.)
   male: 27.45 deaths/1,000 live births

Life expectancy at birth:
   total population: 70.79 years
   male: 68.1 years
   female: 73.61 years (2003 est.)

Total fertility rate: 2.25 children born/woman (2003 est.)

HIV/AIDS—adult prevalence rate: NA

HIV/AIDS—people living with HIV/AIDS: NA

HIV/AIDS—deaths: NA

Nationality:
   noun: Korean(s)
   adjective: Korean

Ethnic groups: racially homogeneous; there is a small Chinese community and a few ethnic Japanese

Religions: traditionally Buddhist and Confucianist, some Christian and syncretic Chondogyo (Religion of the Heavenly Way)

   note: autonomous religious activities now almost nonexistent; government-sponsored religious groups exist to provide illusion of religious freedom

Languages: Korean

Literacy:
   definition: age 15 and over can read and write Korean
   total population: 99%
   male: 99%
   female: 99%

Government

Country name:
   conventional long form: Democratic People's Republic of Korea
   conventional short form: North Korea
   local short form: none
   local long form: Choson-minjujuui-inmin-konghwaguk

note: the North Koreans generally use the term "Choson" to refer to their country
abbreviation: DPRK

Government type: authoritarian socialist; one-man dictatorship

Capital: Pyongyang

Administrative divisions: 9 provinces (do, singular and plural) and 4 special cities* (si, singular and plural); Chagang-do (Chagang Province), Hamgyong-bukto (North Hamgyong Province), Hamgyong-namdo (South Hamgyong Province), Hwanghae-bukto (North Hwanghae Province), Hwanghae-namdo (South Hwanghae Province), Kaesong-si* (Kaesong City), Kangwon-do (Kangwon Province), Najin Sonbong-si*, Namp'o-si* (Namp'o City), P'yongan-bukto (North P'yongan Province), P'yongan-namdo (South P'yongan Province), P'yongyang-si* (Pyongyang City), Yanggang-do (Yanggang Province)

Independence: 15 August 1945 (from Japan)

National holiday: Founding of the Democratic People's Republic of Korea (DPRK), 9 September (1948)

Constitution: adopted 1948, completely revised 27 December 1972, revised again in April 1992 and September 1998

Legal system: based on German civil law system with Japanese influences and Communist legal theory; no judicial review of legislative acts; has not accepted compulsory ICJ jurisdiction

Suffrage: 17 years of age; universal

Executive branch:
chief of state: KIM Jong-il (since NA July 1994); note—on 3 September 2003, KIM Jong-il was reelected Chairman of the National Defense Commission, a position accorded the nation's "highest administrative authority"; KIM Yong-nam was reelected President of the Supreme People's Assembly Presidium and given the responsibility of representing the state and receiving diplomatic credentials
elections: premier elected by the Supreme People's Assembly; election last held NA September 1998 (next to be held NA)
election results: HONG Song-nam elected premier; percent of Supreme People's Assembly vote—NA%
cabinet: Cabinet (Naegak), members, except for the Minister of People's Armed Forces, are appointed by the Supreme People's Assembly
head of government: Premier PAK Pong-chu (since 3 September 2003); Vice Premiers KWAK Pom-ki (since 5 September 1998), CHON Sung-hun (since 3 September 2003), NO Tu-chol (since 3 September 2003)

Legislative branch: unicameral Supreme People's Assembly or Ch'oego Inmin Hoeui (687 seats; members elected by popular vote to serve five-year terms)

elections: last held 3 August 2003 (next to be held in August 2008)

election results: percent of vote by party—NA; seats by party—NA; the KWP approves a list of candidates who are elected without opposition; some seats are held by minor parties

Judicial branch: Central Court (judges are elected by the Supreme People's Assembly)

Political parties and leaders: Chondoist Chongu Party [YU Mi-yong, chairwoman]; Social Democratic Party [KIM Yong-tae, chairman]; major party - Korean Workers' Party or KWP [KIM Jong-il, general secretary]

Political pressure groups and leaders: NA

International organization participation: ARF (dialogue partner), ESCAP, FAO, G-77, ICAO, ICRM, IFAD, IFRCS, IHO, IMO, IOC, ISO, ITU, NAM, UN, UNCTAD, UNESCO, UNIDO, UPU, WFTU, WHO, WIPO, WMO, WToO

Diplomatic representation in the U.S.:

none; note—North Korea has a Permanent Mission to the U.N. in New York

Diplomatic representation from the U.S.:

none (Swedish Embassy in P'yongyang represents the U.S. as consular protecting power)

Flag description: three horizontal bands of blue (top), red (triple width), and blue; the red band is edged in white; on the hoist side of the red band is a white disk with a red five-pointed star

Economy

Overview: North Korea, one of the world's most centrally planned and isolated economies, faces desperate economic conditions. Industrial capital stock is nearly beyond repair as a result of years of under investment and spare parts shortages. Industrial and power output have declined in parallel. The nation has suffered its tenth year of food shortages because of a lack of arable land; collective farming; weather-related problems, including major drought in 2000; and chronic shortages of fertilizer and fuel. Massive international food aid deliveries have allowed the regime to escape mass starvation since 1995–96, but the population remains the victim of prolonged malnutrition and deteriorating living conditions. Large-scale military spending eats up resources needed for investment and civilian consumption. Recently, the regime has placed emphasis on earning hard currency, developing information technology, addressing power shortages, and attracting foreign aid, but in no way at the expense of relinquishing central control over key national assets or undergoing widespread market-oriented reforms. In 2003, heightened political tensions with key donor countries and general donor fatigue have held down the flow of desperately needed food aid and have threatened fuel aid as well.

GDP: purchasing power parity—$22.26 billion (2002 est.)

GDP—real growth rate: 1% (2002 est.)

GDP—per capita: purchasing power parity—$1,000 (2002 est.)

GDP—composition by sector:
agriculture: 30.4%
industry: 32.3%
services: 37.3% (2000 est.)

Population below poverty line: NA%

Household income or consumption by percentage share:
lowest 10%: NA%
highest 10%: NA%

Inflation rate (consumer prices): NA%

Labor force: 9.6 million

Labor force—by occupation: agricultural 36%, nonagricultural 64%

Unemployment rate: NA%

Budget:
revenues: $NA
expenditures: $NA, including capital expenditures of $NA

Industries: military products; machine building, electric power, chemicals; mining (coal, iron ore, magnesite, graphite, copper, zinc, lead, and precious metals), metallurgy; textiles, food processing; tourism

Industrial production growth rate: NA%

Electricity—production: 30.01 billion kWh (2001)

Electricity—production by source:
fossil fuel: 29%
hydro: 71%
other: 0% (2001)
nuclear: 0%

Electricity—consumption: 27.91 billion kWh (2001)

Electricity—exports: 0 kWh (2001)

Electricity—imports: 0 kWh (2001)

Oil—production: 0 bbl/day (2001 est.)

Oil—consumption: 85,000 bbl/day (2001 est.)

Oil—exports: NA (2001)

Oil—imports: NA (2001)

Agriculture—products: rice, corn, potatoes, soybeans, pulses; cattle, pigs, pork, eggs

Exports: $842 million f.o.b. (2001 est.)

Exports—commodities: minerals, metallurgical products, manufactures (including armaments); textiles and fishery products

Exports—partners: China 23.5%, Japan 19.9%, Costa Rica 12.4%, Brazil 6.5% (2002)

Imports: $1.314 billion c.i.f. (2001 est.)

Imports—commodities: petroleum, coking coal, machinery and equipment; textiles, grain

Imports—partners: China 24.9%, Brazil 12.1%, India 9.2%, Thailand 9.2%, Germany 7.8%, Japan 7.1%, Singapore 4.5%, Qatar 4% (2002)

Debt—external: $12 billion (1996 est.)

Economic aid—recipient: $NA; note—nearly $300 million in food aid alone from U.S., South Korea, Japan, and EU in 2001 plus much additional aid from the U.N. and non-governmental organizations

Currency: North Korean won (KPW)

Currency code: KPW

Exchange rates: official: North Korean won per U.S. dollar—150 (December 2002), 2.15 (December 2001), 2.15 (May 1994), 2.13 (May 1992), 2.14 (September 1991), 2.1 (January 1990); market: North Korean won per U.S. dollar—300–600 (December 2002), 200 (December 2001)

Fiscal year: calendar year

Communications

Telephones—main lines in use: 1.1 million (1997)

Telephones—mobile cellular: NA

Telephone system:
general assessment: NA
domestic: NA
international: satellite earth stations—1 Intelsat (Indian Ocean) and 1 Russian (Indian Ocean region); other international connections through Moscow and Beijing

Radio broadcast stations: AM 16, FM 14, shortwave 12 (1999)

Radios: 3.36 million (1997)

Television broadcast stations: 38 (1999)

Televisions: 1.2 million (1997)

Internet country code: .kp

Internet Service Providers (ISPs): 1 (2000)

Internet users: NA

Transportation

Railways:
  total: 5,214 km
  standard gauge: 4,549 km 1.435-m gauge (3,500 km electrified)
  narrow gauge: 665 km 0.762-m gauge (2002)

Highways:
  total: 31,200 km
  paved: 1,997 km
  unpaved: 29,203 km (1999 est.)

Waterways: 2,253 km
  note: mostly navigable by small craft only

Pipelines: oil 136 km (2003)

Ports and harbors: Ch'ongjin, Haeju, Hungnam (Hamhung), Kimch'aek, Kosong, Najin, Namp'o, Sinuiju, Songnim, Sonbong (formerly Unggi), Ungsang, Wonsan

Merchant marine:
  total: 149 ships (1,000 GRT or over) 881,276 GRT/1,309,547 DWT
  note: includes some foreign-owned ships registered here as a flag of convenience: Denmark 1, Greece 2, Pakistan 1, Singapore 1 (2002 est.)
  ships by type: bulk 8, cargo 120, combination bulk 2, container 1, multi-functional large-load carrier 1, passenger 2, passenger/cargo 1, petroleum tanker 8, refrigerated cargo 4, short-sea passenger 2

Airports: 72 (2002)

Airports—with paved runways:
  total: 34
  over 3,047 m: 5
  2,438 to 3,047 m: 18
  1,524 to 2,437 m: 5
  914 to 1,523 m: 3
  under 914 m: 3 (2002)

Airports—with unpaved runways:
  total: 38
  2,438 to 3,047 m: 2
  1,524 to 2,437 m: 18
  914 to 1,523 m: 11
  under 914 m: 7 (2002)

Military

Military branches: Korean People's Army (includes Army, Navy, Air Force), Civil Security Forces

Military manpower—military age: 18 years of age (2003 est.)

Military manpower—availability: males age 15–49: 6,103,615 (2003 est.)

Military manpower—fit for military service: males age 15–49: 3,654,223 (2003 est.)

Military manpower—reaching military age annually: males: 180,875 (2003 est.)

Military expenditures—dollar figure: $5,217.4 million (FY02)

Military expenditures—percent of GDP: 33.9% (FY02)

Transnational Issues

Disputes—international: with China, certain islands in Yalu and Tumen rivers are in uncontested dispute; a section of boundary around Paektu-san (mountain) is indefinite; China objects to illegal migration of North Koreans into northern China; Military Demarcation Line within the 4-km wide Demilitarized Zone has separated North from South Korea since 1953.

Bibliography

Books

Amsden, Alice H. *Asia's Next Giant: South Korea and Late Industrialization.* New York: Oxford University Press, 1989.

Blair, Clay. *The Forgotten War: America in Korea, 1950–1953.* New York: Times Books, 1988.

Buss, Claude A. *The United States and the Republic of Korea: Background for Policy.* Stanford: Hoover Institution Press, 1982.

Chamberlin, Paul F. *Korea 2010: The Challenges of the New Millennium.* Washington, D.C.: Center for Strategic and International Studies, 2001.

Clough, Ralph N. *Embattled Korea: The Rivalry for International Support.* Boulder, Colo.: Westview Press, 1987.

Cole, David C., and Princeton N. Lyman. *Korean Development: The Interplay of Politics and Economics.* Cambridge: Harvard University Press, 1971.

Cumings, Bruce. *The Origins of the Korean War.* 2 vols. Princeton: Princeton University Press, 1990.

Eckert, Carter, et al. *Korea Old and New: A History.* Seoul: Ilchokak Publishers for Harvard University Press, 1990.

Foley, James A. *Korea's Divided Families: Fifty Years of Separation.* London: Routledge Curzon, 2002.

Gonchanov, Sergei N., John W. Lewis, and Zye Litai. *Uncertain Partners: Stalin, Mao, and the Korean War.* Stanford: Stanford University Press, 1994.

Grajdanzev, Andrew J. *Modern Korea.* New York: Octagon Books, 1978.

Han, Woo-kuen. *The History of Korea.* Honolulu: East-West Center Press, 1971.

Henriksen, Thomas, and Jongryn Mo, eds. *North Korea After Kim Il Sung: Continuity or Change?* Stanford: Hoover Institution Press, 1997.

Henthorn, William. *History of Korea.* New York: The Free Press, 1971.

Jacobs, Norman. *The Korean Road to Modernization and Development.* Urbana: University of Illinois Press, 1985.

Jo, Moon H. *Korean Immigrants and the Challenge of Adjustment.* Westport, Conn.: Greenwood Press, 1999.

Kihl, Young Whan. *Politics and Policies in Divided Korea: Regimes in Contest.* Boulder, Colo.: Westview Press, 1984.

Kim, Bun Woong, David S. Bell, Jr., and Chong Bum Lee, eds. *Administrative Dynamics and Development: The Korean Experience.* Seoul: Kyobo Pub., 1985.

Kim, Dae-Jung. *Three-Stage Approach to Korean Reunification: Focusing on the South-North Co-federal State.* Los Angeles: University of California Press, 1997.

Kim, Han-Kyo, ed. *Studies on Korea: A Scholar's Guide.* Honolulu: Center for Korean Studies, University of Hawaii Press, 1980.

Koh, Byung Chul. *The Foreign Policy Systems of North and South Korea*. Berkeley: University of California Press, 1984.

Kwon, Jene K., ed. *Korean Economic Development*. New York: Greenwood Press, 1990.

Lee, Bong. *The Unfinished War: Korea*. New York: Algora Pub., 2003.

Lee, Chong-Sik. *Japan and Korea: The Political Dimension*. Stanford: Hoover Institution Press, 1985.

Lee, Helie. *In the Absence of Sun: A Korean American Woman's Promise to Reunite Three Lost Generations of Her Family*. New York: Harmony Books, 2002.

—. *Still Life with Rice: A Young American Woman Discovers the Life and Legacy of Her Korean Grandmother*. New York: Scribner, 1996.

Lee, Ki-Baik. *A New History of Korea*. Cambridge: Harvard University Press, 1984.

MacDonald, Donald S. *The Koreans: Contemporary Politics and Society*. Boulder, Colo.: Westview Press, 1988.

Merrill, John. *Korea: The Peninsular Origins of the War*. Newark: University of Delaware Press, 1988.

Moon, Chung-in, and David I. Steinberg, eds. *Kim Dae-jung Government and Sunshine Policy: Promises and Challenges*. Seoul: Yonsei University Press, 1999.

Nahm, Andrew C. *North Korea: Her Past, Reality, and Impression*. Kalamazoo: Center for Korean Studies, Western Michigan University, 1978.

Oberdorfer, Don. *The Two Koreas: A Contemporary History*. New York: Basic Books, 2001.

Pae, Sung Moon. *Korea Leading Developing Nations: Economy, Democracy & Welfare*. Lanham, Md.: University Press of America, 1992.

Reilly, Charles E., Jr. *Korea, 1950–1953: The War That Never Was*. St. Davids, Pa.: In-Person Communications, 2000.

Ridgeway, Matthew B. *Korean War*. New York: Doubleday, 1964.

Sigal, Leon V. *Disarming Strangers: Nuclear Diplomacy with North Korea*. Princeton: Princeton University Press, 1998.

Song, Byung-Nak. *The Rise of Korean Economy*. 3rd ed. New York: Oxford University Press, 2003.

Steinberg, David I., ed. *Korean Attitudes Toward the United States: Changing Dynamics*. Armonk, N.Y.: M. E. Sharpe, 2004.

Steinberg, David I. *Stone Mirror: Reflections on Contemporary Korea*. Norwalk, Conn.: EastBridge, 2002.

Web Sites

This section offers the reader a list of Web sites that can provide additional information on North and South Korea, their history, politics, and economies, as well as up-to-date information on current events taking place on the Korean peninsula. These Web sites also include links to other sites that may be of help or interest. Due to the nature of the Internet, the continued existence of a site is never guaranteed, but at the time of this book's publication, all of these Internet addresses were in operation.

Korea.net
www.korea.net

South Korea's government homepage developed and operated by the Korean Information Service (KOIS), now part of the National Information Agency (NIA). It is designed to provide information in English and Korean on a wide range of issues related to Korea.

The Democratic People's Republic of Korea
http://www.korea-dpr.com/

Official homepage of North Korea. Provides links to informative Web sites on North Korea's history, politics, and society.

Korea Foundation
www.kofo.or.kr

This site offers information on the scope of Foundation programs and activities, as well as useful links to Korea and publications of the Korea Foundation.

Ministry of Finance and Economy
http://english.mofe.go.kr/main.php

This site provides information on the Korean economy, such as statistical data, Korean economic policy issues, and economic indicators.

Korean Statistical Information System
http://www.nso.go.kr/eng/

A Web site providing major statistical information on Korea's population, social indicators, trade, and industry.

The Bank of Korea
http://www.bok.or.kr/

The official Web site of The Bank of Korea, it provides access to statistics about the Korean economy, as well as the country's financial system, payment system, Korean economic-related speeches, and Korean currency.

Korea Institute for Industrial Economics & Trade (KIET)

http://www.kiet.re.kr/e_main.html

Provides access to several databases on South Korean economic information, such as industrial economy and market information.

U.S. Forces Korea

http://www.korea.army.mil/

A Web site discussing U.S. military forces along the DMZ. Provides links to major organizations and personnel units in Korea, as well as other military links. Also provides information informing the public about what is going on in South Korea.

Network Korea

http://www.han.com/

Provides links to different activities in Korea, from entertainment to travel to business.

The Embassy of Korea in the U.S.A.

http://www.koreaembassyusa.org/

Provides news and press releases, information about South Korea–U.S. relations, and facts for traveling to Korea, such as mandatory paperwork, passport information, and embassy locations in South Korea.

The Korea Society

http://www.koreasociety.org/index.htm

The Korea Society's goal is to make more people aware of Korean culture and the present situation on the peninsula. This Web site offers relevant information and activities about Korean history and culture, as well as educational opportunities for students who are interested in learning more about Korea and/or its language.

Korea Web Weekly

http://www.kimsoft.com/korea.htm

Provides weekly news and articles on events on the Korean peninsula. Also provides links to other media outlets supplying Korean news.

Additional Periodical Articles with Abstracts

More information dealing with North and South Korea can be found in the following articles. Readers who require a more comprehensive selection are advised to consult *Readers' Guide to Periodical Literature*, *Readers' Guide Abstracts*, *Business Abstracts*, *Education Abstracts*, *General Science Abstracts*, *Humanities Abstracts*, *Social Sciences Abstracts*, and other H. W. Wilson publications.

The North Korean Conundrum. Nicholas Mele. *America*, v. 189 pp18–20 September 8, 2003.

Mele writes that the news stories about North Korea appear to lurch from saber-rattling toward negotiations and back again. According to Mele, despite the most recent agreement on multiparty talks, mutual misperceptions and avoidance of the issue may yet risk an unnecessary war, whose victims will be the civilian populations of North and South Korea. As all sides prepare to meet, Mele advises the United States and the Democratic People's Republic of Korea to end the mutual name-calling, to stop dismissing Kim Jong Il as irrational, and to consider the realities confronted by all parties concerned with the Korean peninsula.

State Building in North Korea: From a "Self Reliant" to a "Military-First" State. Soyoung Kwon. *Asian Affairs* (London), v. 34 pp286–96 November 2003.

The writer examines the process of state building and political development in North Korea and outlines regime peculiarities and unique elements that distinguish it from other socialist regimes in order to understand the regime in 2003. She argues that North Korea is changing into a military-oriented regime and is utilizing the nuclear and military card in its negotiations with the outside world in such a way that it has been tagged as a dangerous and menacing "rogue state." She assesses how the country became a unique "military" state, overriding its socialist goals, and whether this represents the regime's new survival strategy.

Economic Reform and Military Downsizing: A Key to Solving the North Korean Nuclear Crisis? Michael O'Hanlon and Mike Mochizuki. *Brookings Review*, v. 21 pp12–17 Fall 2003.

According to O'Hanlon and Mochizuki, U.S. policy toward North Korea needs a major overhaul as the country continues to develop a nuclear arsenal. They believe that a grand bargain could be proposed to Pyongyang that would deal with the country's broken economy and other aspects of its failed society. North Korea could be offered a new relationship with the outside world and substantial aid if it would denuclearize, reduce military forces, and move in a direction like that of Vietnam and China in recent decades. Even if the plan failed, they believe that Washington—having seriously attempted diplomacy—would be in a much stronger position to argue to Seoul, Tokyo, and Beijing that tough measures were needed against North Korea. They feel that America has a good chance of succeeding if North Korea wants to make such an aid effort work and if expectations are reasonable.

North Korea: No Bygones at Yongbyon. Robert Alvarez. *The Bulletin of the Atomic Scientists*, v. 59 pp38–45 July/August 2003.

Alvarez explores the crisis that arose between the United States and North Korea when the U.S. confronted North Korea with its knowledge that Pyongyang was secretly developing gas centrifuge technology to enrich uranium for nuclear weapons. Examining the Bush administration's use of capitalizing on the Agreed Framework of 1994s "all or nothing" provision, Alvarez believes that given the flaws in the Agreed Framework, talks among the United States, China, and North Korea could produce a more workable solution.

Sit Down and Talk. Wade L. Huntley. *The Bulletin of the Atomic Scientists*, v. 59 pp28–29+ July/August 2003.

Huntley focuses on the Bush administration's North Korea policy adjustment of accepting Pyongyang's nuclear status and focusing instead on their export activities. North Korea's surprise admission that it had a secret uranium program sparked a cascading breakdown of the U.S.–North Korea Agreed Framework, which had restrained North Korea's plutonium-based nuclear program for almost a decade. Huntley discusses North Korea's termination of international monitoring at the Yongbyon nuclear complex and the preparations undertaken to begin reprocessing the spent fuel that had been stored under the agreement. Huntley concludes by stating that to peacefully attain a nonnuclear North Korea, the Bush administration has no other option but to sit down and negotiate.

Korean Reunification. Sharif M. Shuja. *Contemporary Review*, v. 283 pp65–75 August 2003.

The writer covers the issue of Korean unification from several perspectives. He argues that unity can occur only with economic reforms in the North.

North Korea Under Kim Jong-Il. Sharif M. Shuja. *Contemporary Review*, v. 282 pp200–5 April 2003.

The writer addresses problems facing North Korea (DPRK) and asks whether such a totalitarian system can continue to operate with the same degree of effectiveness and without any major change in the 21st century. Shuja claims that dealing with the reality of the North as it exists and waiting for the country to change gradually may now be the only way to advance. He concludes that four principles should guide Seoul and the West in their approach to Pyongyang: recognition of North Korea as a state, formulation of policies that will encourage internal change, preservation of the regional great power consensus, and the prevention of war at all costs.

The Korea Crisis. Victor D. Cha and David C. Kang. *Foreign Policy*, pp20–24+ May/June 2003.

Cha and Kang discuss the veracity of widely held beliefs about North Korea. North Korea is not mad, about to disintegrate, nor about to begin a war, they claim, but it is dangerous, as well as dangerously misunderstood. Their article focuses on countering the threat that North Korea presents to its neighbors and the world by curtailing bluster, acquiring more patience, and, on the part of the United States, being willing to explore and comprehend the real sources of the North's conduct.

Bad Loans to Good Friends: Money Politics and the Developmental State in South Korea. David C. Kang. *International Organization*, v. 56 pp177–207 Winter 2002.

The writer considers money politics and the developmental state in South Korea. He argues that such politics were widespread in South Korea both during and following the high-growth era the country experienced. Furthermore, he contends that political rather than economic considerations dominated policymaking in the country. He also compares the patterns of money politics that arose in South Korea after the democratic transition in 1987 with those of the early post-independence era.

Financial Liberalization in South Korea. Eundak Kwon. *Journal of Contemporary Asia*, v. 34 pp 70–101 2004.

Kwon analyzes the process of financial liberalization in South Korea from the perspective of financial globalization through an international political economic approach. He explains that Korean financial liberalization has been highly influenced by outside pressure from the United States, the OECD, and the IMF, as well as by the big business conglomerates (chaebols), as a powerful domestic interest group. Kwon examines the two viewpoints—the domestic and the globalization perspectives—held on the causes of the Korean financial crisis of 1997–98.

A Dangerous Game in Korea. Tim Shorrock. *The Nation*, v. 276 pp18–20 January 27, 2003.

American policies fanning anti-Americanism in both North and South Korea are the topic of Shorrock's article. He argues that anti-American sentiment has been steadily increasing in South Korea since the 1980s due to U.S. support for a succession of military dictators as well as its refusal to embrace the yearning for national unification that peaked in 2000, when South Korean president Kim Dae Jung traveled to Pyongyang for the first meeting between the presidents of North and South Korea. Shorrock maintains that many Koreans think that President

Bush's curt dismissal of Kim's "sunshine policy," his inclusion of Pyongyang in his "axis of evil," and his doctrine of preemptive strikes against potential enemies have sent a clear message that America has no interest in a negotiated peace in Korea. South Koreans now go out of their way to tell foreign reporters that they regard the United States as being more dangerous than the police state to their north and even defend North Korea's attempts to develop nuclear weapons.

Living with the Unthinkable: How to Coexist with a Nuclear North Korea. Ted Galen Carpenter. *National Interest*, pp92–98 Winter 2003.

Carpenter asserts that U.S. strategies for dealing with the North Korean nuclear program are based on the assumption that the correct policy mix will result in the country abandoning its nuclear ambitions, an assumption that may be misplaced. In preparing for this possibility, Carpenter advises the U.S. to inform North Korea that it would view Pyongyang's selling of nuclear material to hostile governments or terrorist organizations as a threat to U.S. security. He also says the U.S. should show a willingness to remove economic sanctions on, and extend diplomatic recognition to, North Korea. Such a policy mix, he states, may not produce an ideal outcome, but it is preferable to the alternatives of either attempting to bribe or pressurize Pyongyang to give up its nuclear ambitions, or launching a preemptive war.

Averting the Unthinkable. Stephen J. Morris. *National Interest*, pp99–114 Winter 2003.

According to Morris, if the U.S. is serious about preventing North Korea from developing into a nuclear power, it must accept the need to remove North Korea's regime and its leader, Kim Jong Il, from power. Morris believes that a democratic North Korea would be most conducive to U.S. interests, for both strategic and moral reasons, though an authoritarian dictatorship based on the Chinese model, and committed to social and economic reforms, would also be acceptable.

Island Getaway. *The New Republic*, v. 227 pp9 December 30, 2002.

This article discusses Washington's potential ability to bring down North Korean leader Kim Jong Il by promoting a huge flow of refugees from his country. It argues that America should revamp immigration laws to welcome North Korean refugees as asylum-seekers at U.S. embassies and borders, and Congress should launch a joint fact-finding mission with the Japanese, South Koreans, and Europeans to garner information from North Koreans in China about the human rights abuses they endured. According to the article, President Bush and the leaders of European nations, which have diplomats on the ground in Pyongyang, ought to speak out more aggressively on these matters. The article admits that a pro-exodus policy will take time, but insists that an imperfect North Korean policy is better than none at all.

New Deal. Peter Maass. *The New Republic*, v. 229 pp16–19 December 22, 2003.

Peter Maass examines the battle between hard-liners who want to topple Kim Jong Il as rapidly as possible and moderates who want to give him an opportunity to swap his nuclear program for aid. While neither side admits to any other options, Maass asserts that a third choice does in fact exist: putting pressure on Kim while constraining the threats of war and proliferation. Maass discusses this option as well as the three elements required to implement it successfully.

A Riddle Wrapped in an Enigma. Howard W. French. *New York Times Upfront*, v. 135 pp14–16+ December 13, 2002.

French discusses the troubled state of North Korea, including a series of devastating droughts and floods that have led to major crop failures and widespread famine and starvation. He considers how the country relies heavily on international food aid to feed its starving population, but it spends a huge amount of money to maintain an army of around 1 million soldiers and a nuclear-weapons program that has resulted in the country's inclusion in President Bush's "axis of evil." French addresses North Korea's admission of a nuclear-weapons program which has stymied recent reform efforts and resulted in economic sanctions, adding to the country's already desperate circumstances. French also examines North Korea's inability to afford either fuel or spare parts to maintain its industries, which leads experts to believe that the country's factories are operating at no more than 10 percent of their capacity.

South Korea's Search for a Unification Strategy. Seongji Woo. *Orbis*, v. 47 pp511–25 Summer 2003.

While addressing the issue of rivalry between South and North Korea, which has been ongoing since the 1950s, the writer focuses on South Korea's attempt at a full engagement policy toward its counterpart. Woo argues that for South Korea, a comprehensive engagement policy equipped with a mechanism to compel the North's compliance with certain vital terms is the best and perhaps only way to achieve Korean unification and integration. When the nuclear issue on the Korean peninsula is resolved, Woo believes that this current reconciliation could potentially go deeper and last longer than past such efforts by the two countries.

Cutting the Tripwire. Doug Bandow. *Reason*, v. 35 pp34–38 July 2003.

Bandow claims that the only reason Washington is entangled in the Korean peninsula is because it has defended South Korea for 50 years. He contends that the alliance with the Republic of Korea has been America's most consistently dangerous commitment since World War II and is the only reason North Korea breathes fire against Washington. Asserting his belief that alliances are formed at particular times to meet specific threats and are not ends in themselves to be preserved no matter what, Bandow advocates a complete U.S. troop withdrawal, thereby neutralizing Pyongyang's threat to America, and ultimately turning over the problem to North Korea's neighbors.

Handling North Korea: Strategy and Issues. Shik Choo Yong. *SAIS Review*, v. 23 pp43–51 Winter/Spring 2003.

Shik Choo Yong addresses the perceptions held among Americans about North Korea, its regime, and prospects for its future, which have been the driving force behind establishing North Korean policies. Handling Pyongyang includes dealing with various critical issues, such as weapons of mass destruction, human rights violations, Korean unification, the U.S.–ROK alliance, and stability in East Asia. Those issues, according to the writer, must be carefully prioritized for any effective coordination between Washington and Seoul. The writer believes that engagement or containment alone will not untangle these complex issues, and a more cautious, gradual, and selective approach is required.

Korea: A House Divided. Jonathan Kandell. *Smithsonian*, v. 34 pp38–44+ July 2003.

Kandell examines the history of North and South Korea and the emergence of the North as a potential nuclear threat to the South. He discusses the roughly 700,000 North Korean soldiers spread along the Demilitarized Zone (DMZ) that divides the Korean peninsula, capable of devastating Seoul, only 25 miles away, and the recent escalation of tensions as North Korea proclaims it has the capacity to build a nuclear bomb. Kandell assesses the contrasting economic situations in both countries, including the growing economic crisis in the North, which has resulted in widespread starvation and an energy shortage.

Focus on the Future, Not the North. Victor D. Cha. *Washington Quarterly*, v. 26 pp91–107 Winter 2002.

Cha focuses on the alliance between the U.S. and South Korea, which has been steadily approaching a pivotal reassessment, as concerns have been raised over North Korea's uranium—enriched facilities, the U.S. military presence in the region, the direction of the U.S.–South Korea alliance, and the need to prepare for the contingency of Korean unification. The writer believes that it is time to stop thinking about the alliance in ad hoc terms and to start creating the vision for the future U.S. presence in Northeast Asia generally and on the Korean peninsula specifically.

Anti-Americanism in Korea. Seung-Hwan Kim. *Washington Quarterly*, v. 26 pp109–22 Winter 2002.

Seung-Hwan Kim addresses the anti-Americanism that has been growing at a startling rate in South Korea and has spread to almost all strata of Korean society. The reasons for this growing unpopularity and resentment are complex and diverse, Kim believes, ranging from dissatisfaction with President George W.

Bush's harsh "axis of evil" rhetoric toward North Korea, since September 11, 2001; the continued presence of U.S. military bases on Korean soil; Korea's changing demographic structure; rising nationalism; the fear that the U.S. may abandon South Korea in favor of global strategic interests; and the negative portrayal of America in the Korean media. The writer argues that unless Washington and Seoul work together to stem this tide of discontent through some kind of public outreach campaign that will help to improve the U.S. image, popular Korean attitudes could jeopardize the future of the U.S.–Korean alliance.

China and the Korean Peninsula: Playing for the Long Term. David Shambaugh. *Washington Quarterly*, v. 26 pp43–56 Spring 2003.

China's policy toward North Korea is detailed in Shambaugh's article. In 2003 President George W. Bush and other world leaders sought the assistance of the Chinese government in halting North Korea's nuclear program. Despite China's policy in favor of a nonnuclear Korean peninsula, halting North Korea's nuclear program has not been China's ultimate goal, argues Shambaugh. China's aims in relation to the Korean peninsula are more long term and more complicated, he believes, and the U.S. and other nations must understand these perspectives and complexities if they are to successfully gain China's cooperation on the issue.

How to Build a Nation. David Ekbladh. *The Wilson Quarterly*, v. 28 pp12–16+ Winter 2004.

Ekbladh outlines the history of U.S. involvement in Korea, which began in the aftermath of World War II. He asserts that when Americans entered Korea nearly 60 years ago with the aim of creating a modern nation, they could not have imagined how successful they would be or how long it would take to effect change. Ekbladh explains that no one foresaw the scale of commitment required by the U.S., as some 37,000 U.S. troops still remain on the Korean peninsula facing a hostile North Korean regime. Ekbladh discusses the contingent factors surrounding U.S. aid, as well as the perseverance and initiatives taken on the part of the South Koreans, which led to their prosperity and freedom after an immense and protracted effort.

Rethinking the East Asian Balance of Power: Historical Antagonism, Internal Balancing, and the Korean-Japanese Security Relationship. Jihwan Hwang. *World Affairs*, v. 166 pp95–108 Fall 2003.

The historical legacy that exists between Japan and South Korea is used to explain the troubled and turbulent relationship between the two countries in Hwang's article. Hwang argues that the historical antagonism between the two has prevented South Korea from attempting to develop security cooperation with Japan, and has also influenced Japan's security policy. Hwang examines how the two countries opted to respond to the military crisis during the 1970s through internal military buildups rather than through external security cooperation. Thus, suggests Hwang, because of the colonial legacy.

"One Rogue State Crisis at a Time!" The United States and North Korea's Nuclear Weapons Program. Terence Roehrig. *World Affairs*, v. 165 pp155–78 Spring 2003.

Roehrig discusses the DPRK deputy foreign minister Kang Sok Joo's confirmation following meetings between representatives from the U.S. and the Democratic People's Republic of Korea (DPRK) held in Pyongyang, North Korea, on October 3–5, 2002, that his country had begun a second effort to develop nuclear weapons. Roehrig also assesses the implications of Joo's indication that should the U.S. guarantee not to attack the North, complete a peace treaty with North Korea, and accept the North's sovereignty, then North Korea would be prepared to give up its nuclear weapons program.

Index

951.   THE TWO KOREAS
904
TWO